From TWO-STROKE
to TURBO

From TWO-STROKE to TURBO

SAAB in motorsport since 1949

ANDERS TUNBERG

First published in Sweden by PMP AB/RALLYSPORT, UPPSALA
Copyright © 1980 — Anders Tunberg

English language edition published 1980 by
MOTOR RACING PUBLICATIONS LTD
28 Devonshire Road, Chiswick, London W4 2HD, England

ISBN 0 900549 57 2

Printed in Great Britain by The Garden City Press Limited,
Letchworth, Hertfordshire SG6 1JS.

Colour separations and printing by The Purchasing Link Limited,
Warlingham, Surrey.

Contents

Foreword		7
1	A flying start	9
2	'You couldn't let up — ever'	16
3	Three cylinders are better than two	20
4	Harald's five tough months	23
5	Lots of medals — in racing	27
6	The Saab Sonett — so neat	34
7	The toughest ever	37
8	A Saab at Le Mans	41
9	Safari — the missing victory	44
10	The professionals in Monte Carlo	51
11	Formula cars without success	58
12	Ten victories out of 29 starts	61
13	Carl-Magnus Skogh — a true finisher	68
14	The RAC Rally — one of the best	71
15	From 25 to 250 horsepower	78
16	Baja — 1,000 miles in 20 hours	88
17	Nobody drops a rear axle anymore	93
18	Blue and white — for Finland	98
19	Good neighbours?	101
20	Rallycross — all action	106
21	From Little Le Mans to Showroom Stocks	111
22	Into the 'eighties	119
	Saab rally success record	123
	Saab rally car standard specifications	125

The publishers wish to acknowledge the following photographers whose work has contributed to the pictorial content of this book: Odd H Anthonsen, Hugh Bishop, Holger Eklund, Svante Fischerström, Nils-Olof Johansson, Rolf Kukacka, Alf Lavér, Per Lidström, Antero Lindell, Lars-Olof Magnil, Göte Nyman, Ingemar Nyström, Kalle Riggare, Hans Sandström, Colin Taylor Productions, Göran Thobiasson and Roland Thyberg.

Foreword

When SAAB started planning postwar production in the mid-forties it was realized that cars would be in great demand after the war. But cars were something quite new to SAAB and there was no test track available where prototypes could be tested. Thus, the first cars were run at night around Trollhättan and the experience gained on the secondary back roads formed the basis of the car to come — the Saab 92.

This was the most simple way of testing if practice could match the theories. Many of the technicians were active rally or racing drivers and they knew what you had to demand of a car built for the Swedish roads.

By the end of 1949 production had started and at the same time SAAB wrote the first page of its now 30-year-old rally history. The debut was in the Östergötland Runt, less than one month after production had started, and the driver — K. G. Svedberg — won the event outright. Since then, Saab drivers have won many victories, and have lost on even more occasions.

But we who work with SAAB have never complained about being beaten. Instead, we have tried to learn from our mistakes. Technical shortcomings have been quickly corrected and, as a result, the production cars have been improved. This has given a meaning to our competition activities.

Thirty years is a long time. New car makes have appeared on the rallying scene, only to disappear again some years later. But SAAB has been there all the time — and that is unique, for no other manufacturer has been active in rallying for as long as SAAB.

At SAAB we believe in rallying when it comes to speeding up technical development. This is one of the reasons why we have always tried to keep our rally cars as standard as possible.

But how did it all begin?

Who were the drivers?

And how is it today?

Some of us might remember what happened in the fifties, and now Anders Tunberg helps us to fill in the missing parts. I do hope you will enjoy this book as much as I did.

Sten Wennlo

Sten Wennlo
(Managing Director, Saab Car Division)

Chapter 1

A flying start

On April 25, 1949, the assembly line at the SAAB Trollhättan factory started rolling, and by the end of the day the first of 20 pre-series Saab 92s was standing proudly inside the factory.

The company's history dates back another 12 years, though, to 1937, when Svenska Aeroplan AB (SAAB) began producing aeroplanes for the Swedish Air force. During the thirties it became increasingly obvious to the Swedish Government that war would eventually break out and the establishment of SAAB ensured that Sweden would not be dependent on the western allies for air defence.

By 1944 it was apparent that the war was drawing towards a close and it became necessary for SAAB to diversify its manufacturing capacity in order to survive. After looking at many projects, including prefabricated buildings, the SAAB management decided that the company's design and engineering skills lay more in the direction of car manufacturing, and it was to this end that Project 92 was born.

The main objectives for the designers were: low weight, an aerodynamically efficient design, fuel economy, front-wheel drive, durability and strength. Leading the Project 92 design team was chief engineer Gunnar Ljungström, aided by Sixten Sason.

The first Saab car, chassis number 92001, was produced in 1946 and was followed in 1947 by test cars two, three and four. In all, those cars were test-driven for 170,000 miles, but although the people at SAAB's headquarters in Linköping had proved themselves excellent engineers they lacked in sales ability.

All was not lost, however, for Sweden's largest car dealer — Gunnar V. Philipson — not only ordered the first 8,000 Saabs due to be produced,

but, it is said, he also paid for them in advance. It was this down-payment which aided SAAB's severe lack of finance and its cash-flow problems, and without Philipson's personal commitment the Saab's rally debut would not have come about as early as it did. Series production started in December 1949, with prospective buyers queueing up to get the cars. One story says that Philipson had signed orders for 35,000 cars following the 92's public debut at the S:t Erik Fair in the autumn of 1949 — a slight exaggeration, but the interest was enormous.

Barely a couple of weeks after production started, K. G. Svedberg, a sales manager and part-time rally driver from one of Philipson's dealerships, drove a Saab 92 in the Tour of Östergötland rally. He won the event, and little did he know that that victory was to be the first of so many.

That impressive first victory was enough to convince the Norwegian rallying star Greta Molander that she should drive a Saab 92 in her tenth Monte Carlo Rally. Backing for the venture came from Gunnar V. Philipson, who decided that a two-car team would have a better chance of success. This was not Greta's first drive for Philipson, for in the past she had rallied Dodges and DKWs for him.

The two cars, chassis numbers 92007 and 92008, were prepared under the supervision of Rolf Mellde, who was one of SAAB's engine designers, and whose knowledge enabled him to increase output of the engines to 35 bhp — 10 bhp more than standard. Inside, the cars were equipped with stopwatches, map-reading lights, etc, while the co-driver's seat could be folded down, although this facility was barely used in the tough 2,000-mile trek across Europe.

Both cars started from Stockholm, Greta

Molander and her partner, Margaretha von Essen, in car number 152, and K. G. Svedberg and Rolf Mellde in car number 162. Snow was the biggest hazard, especially as studded tyres and snow chains were banned. After 1,800 miles of virtually non-stop driving the competitors came to the first selective (speed test) between Digne and Grasse — the most difficult part of the classic *Route Napoleon* — where the average speed, even in those far-off days, was 40 mph. Of the 280 starters only 135, including the Saabs, reached the finish within the time limit. Although neither Saab qualified for the final 10.5-miles *Grande Corniche* test, Greta Molander still finished 55th overall, eighth in class and second in the ladies' class, while newcomers Svedberg and Mellde finished 69th overall.

Thirty years on, the drivers can look back to that first Monte as a joke, especially as they had been lucky to finish because both cars had suffered engine bearing problems. Nevertheless, that joke created a lot of publicity for the embryonic car company and also provided a lot of technical information.

The following summer saw the first Swedish Rally to the Midnight Sun, organized by the Royal Swedish Automobile Club. The event was initiated by Ernst Nilson, Sweden's main Volvo dealer, who wanted to see foreign rally drivers competing in Sweden when the country was at its scenic best.

The event had two starting points, Falsterbo, in southern Sweden, and Stockholm, with the two routes merging at Örebro. From there the competitors headed north to Kiruna, in Lapland. Special tests *en route* decided the outcome of the event, but despite the low 31 mph average for the road sections and the 46 mph demanded on the special tests many of the competitors didn't make the finish line. Pehr-Fredrik Cederbaum won the event in a BMW while the German, Prince Joachim von Fürstenberg, driving a Porsche, won the class in which Rolf Mellde and Ragnar Åke Carlsson entered their Saab. Nevertheless, second in class was not to be scorned at in an event where classes were defined by engine capacity.

Per Nyström — father of Pat Moss' co-driver Elisabeth Nyström — and F. Hedman were seventh and ninth in class, respectively. It was a long time, however, before anything other than a sports or GT car would win this event; as we will learn later on, SAAB had to build the Sonett sports car before they had any real chance of winning, although in the end the Sonett wasn't needed as the rules were changed overnight when the car was introduced.

Although SAAB were not winning all the rallies they entered, drivers such as Mellde, Svedberg, Molander and Nyström were proving that the 92 was a tough car. And, because Mellde was in charge of development, any shortcomings which

competition activities highlighted were quickly overcome and production cars were suitably modified. This rapid transfer of technical data from competition to production line is a philosophy that SAAB have followed carefully, as they believe emphatically that competition really does improve the breed.

During 1950, Rolf Mellde entered a few minor rallies in preparation for the big one — the Rikspokalen. Although the Monte Carlo and Swedish rallies were both longer, the Rikspokalen was considered to be Europe's toughest rally during the thirties and fifties.

The 'roads' were little more than tracks through forests and across farms, and barely plotted on the 1:100,000-scale maps used. The navigation, though, was easy compared with the average speeds which were demanded by the organizers.

The start was scheduled for 6 pm on Saturday, November 18, but even before the first car got away snow began to fall and the organizers reduced the average speed by 10 per cent to 28 mph. The

Greta Molander with Rolf Mellde, who began the long and successful story of Saabs in competition when they entered the 1950 Monte Carlo Rally.

For the first Swedish Rally to the Midnight Sun Saabs were driven by Rolf Mellde (in the car) and Pelle Nyström (alongside).

Singer team withdrew because of the adverse weather and other teams rushed around to find winter tyres. Those who started did so with an odd selection of tyres, and one driver — Oscar Swahn — had Wiresoles airfreighted from England specially for the event (these tyres had vulcanized wires set in the rubber). Rolf Mellde started with ordinary winter tyres, those on the front being fitted with chains. Even so, he spun several times on the special stages, but still managed to keep the 92 going.

Thousands of spectators gathered along the route to watch the desperate efforts of the competitors to keep their cars going through the ice and snow, which badly impaired visibility. Although service cars were forbidden, clandestine servicing was taking place — even in those days! — the only legal assistance allowed being for tyre changes. The freezing weather created its own hazards, notably frozen petrol pipes and carburettors, iced-up windscreens and frequent battery changes — in one instance as many as five were changed.

Through all this, Rolf Mellde plugged his way to overall victory — the first major win for the marque. According to Mellde it was nothing short of a miracle, helped by the right choice of tyres and Mellde's confidence to run the Saab flat out where others hesitated lest their cars break.

The Rikspokalen proved to be a SAAB walk-over, which included outright victory, the manufacturer's team prize (Mellde, Svedberg and Molander) and the ladies' prize (Greta Molander, who else?), while Mellde was also in the winning club team. The Saab had arrived. Mellde's reward for victory? He was paid just 300 crowns (about £30 in those days)!

SAAB's international breakthrough, though, was thwarted on numerous occasions, starting with Rolf Mellde's entry in the 1951 Monte Carlo Rally. His co-driver, this time, was Ragnar Carlsson, a SAAB test driver, and by the time the duo had reached the French Alps they had a commanding lead over the rest of the field, but this disappeared when the engine started to misfire — they had run out of fuel. Luckily for them they carried a spare can and they were able to continue, only for the car

Rolf Mellde and co-driver Bengt Carlqvist (right) won the first important victory by a Saab in the Rikspokalen in 1950.

to stop again. After checking the car's electrics, Mellde discovered that the carburettor was iced up. The potential winners were to end up lost amongst the tail-enders and, to this day, nobody seems to know their final placing. There was, however, some little consolation in Greta Molander's fourth place in the ladies' class.

On his return to Sweden, Mellde developed and fitted a preheating device for the Saab's intake manifold to prevent icing-up occuring again. As far as is known, SAAB were pioneers in this field.

On home ground, SAAB weren't quite so fortunate as they were competing against Volkswagens powered by 1,300 cc Porsche engines producing 75 bhp. In the unofficial championship, Mellde came 11th overall, while SAAB were second to Volkswagen in the manufacturers' championship.

In 1951 the SAAB team went all-out to win the Rikspokalen rally for the second year running and entered six cars, but it was not to be enough; the best they could do was Gösta Begqvist third, Mellde fourth and Svedberg eighth.

13

Greta Molander was the cover girl of rallying in the early-fifties and won the ladies' prize in the Monte Carlo Rally several times.

The first official rally championship took place in 1952, when both Volkswagen and Austin entered works teams supported by plenty of post-event publicity. SAAB were very much the poor relations, but the small car gave their drivers a moral advantage and when victory came it was that much sweeter. The first championship ended in overall victory for Gunnar Källström (father of the great Harry 'Sputnik' Källström), with Mellde finishing a lowly 24th and beaten by Kronegård (eighth) and Svedberg (ninth) overall. The rules were changed at the end of that first championship, banning the use of special tyres, and VW promised to use standard engines rather than the Porsche units. It is worth mentioning that a young hopeful called Bo Hellberg won the navigator's championship that year; ten years later he was to become head of SAAB's Competition's Department.

One of the Saab 92s heading through the night towards Monte Carlo.

Chapter 2

'You couldn't let up — ever'

Rallying myths are often born in bars as enthusiasts and competitors swop drinks and stories, and one of Sweden's rallying myths proclaimed that 'when it is really twisty the Saab is at its best'. How untrue, since twisty roads demand good acceleration out of corners, something the little two-strokes didn't possess, and in fact a characteristic that Saabs didn't really have until the introduction of the Turbo in 1978.

Volkswagen were *the* rally cars in those early days, the four-speed gearbox giving their drivers a distinct advantage over those piloting the three-speed Saabs.

'You couldn't let up — ever,' Erik Carlsson says, 'you had to brake with the left foot at the same time as you kept your right foot on the accelerator. This was not some sort of finesse that we learned to get the tail out in the bends. More important than that was to keep the revs up in order to get quickly out of the bends.'

Against all the odds, Rolf Mellde won the championship in 1953, when three years of trying paid off with three straight victories — more than enough to keep the Volkswagen-engined (as distinct from Porsche-engined) VWs at bay.

Erik Carlsson's rallying career had started in 1952 when he entered that year's Swedish Rally as co-driver to Per Nyström. Because of weight distribution problems, Erik sat in the rear seat of the Volvo 444N (!) (some 26 years later Fiat did the same thing when Christian Geistdorfer was co-driving for Walter Rohrl in their Fiat 131 on the RAC Rally).

The overall effect on Erik was disastrous since he was violently sick into Per's hat — it being the nearest container to hand.

In spite of this inauspicious debut, Erik sold his motorcross bike and bought a secondhand Saab 92 from a farmer. Carlsson's first rally was with Sten Helm as navigator and, despite Erik's 'Junior B' licence, he tried to emulate more senior drivers, keeping his right foot firmly planted on the accelerator. Eventually enthusiasm overtook skill and on landing from a long jump the battery tore itself loose and Erik's car left the track backwards through a hedge; fortunately, Helm was an electrician and got the car going again. On the Monday following the rally, Erik presented himself at Mellde's Trollhättan office, begging parts for his green Saab, and Mellde gave them to him.

From that time on Erik made frequent visits to the SAAB plant to collect bits of bodywork and the like that he found on the grass outside the fence. . . .

Erik won the local championship in 1954, amongst other things, not because of the car but due more to his persistence, willpower and sheer bravery.

Rallying in Sweden in the fifties was still dominated by VW, SAAB's success coming abroad. In 1955, Rolf Mellde found himself leading the Tulip Rally until the final test at Zandvoort where a bearing seized. Choking the car fiercely, Mellde managed to get as much fuel oil as possible into the crankcase and eventually finished second behind Maurice Gatsonides' TR2. Greta Molander won the ladies' class, SAAB the manufacturers' team prize, with Sunbeam-Talbot second.

Admittedly, the Saab now produced all of 28 bhp compared to its original 25 bhp, but the engine was still severely lacking in power. But in the pipeline was the new Saab 93, complete with a three-cylinder, 748 cc, 33 bhp power unit.

The 92's last victory as a works car was the 1955

Rolf Mellde and Bengt Carlqvist gave SAAB their first Swedish Championship driving the legendary P 9101 during the 1953 season.

Rikspokalen in the hands of Erik Carlsson. Erik drove the tough 500-miles event in the same car that Mellde had used for the Tulip Rally. Despite all the snow, Erik refused to use tyre chains as they slowed the car down too much, while to make matters worse the heater was incapable of keeping the windscreen clear of ice and Erik had to peer out of the side windows to see where he was going!

By the last stage, he was so far in the lead he could afford to take a coffee break — his reputation now secure. Rolf Mellde even flew from Trollhättan to Stockholm to congratulate the victorious Carlsson, then, on December 7, 1955, SAAB entered a new era with the introduction of the 93.

The Tour d'Europe was the Marathon of the fifties and involved 13,000 kilometres in 13 days. Rolf Mellde was partnered by motoring journalist Sverker Benson and took second place overall in a well-equipped Saab 93.

Pause at a check point during the Tour d'Europe.

Good use was made of pockets on the doors of the Saab 93 for the essential aids for endurance rallying.

Chapter 3

Three cylinders are better than two

With the introduction of the more powerful 93, SAAB finally had the machinery to win international rallies. On January 1, 1956, the company managed to get an exemption from the production minimum for standard cars — a rare occurrence in those days — and a month later the Trollhättan enthusiasts had got the car sorted out to their liking so that soon the Saab 93 was starting to dominate ice races as well as rallies. In the first qualifier for that year's championship — and the 93's first rally — Ivar Andersson came second, Carl-Magnus Skogh fifth and Erik Carlsson eighth. On the second event Erik Carlsson earned his nickname 'På taket', (literally translated it means 'On the roof') by a fellow competitor who had seen Erik roll his car off the stage. When asked if he had seen Erik, the driver replied, 'You mean Carlsson on the roof?' after a popular children's radio programme of that name. Ever since then 'På taket' has appeared on Erik's rally cars.

On April 18, the 93 was homologated as a standard production car just in time for the Tulip Rally where Sture Nottorp/Charlie Lohmander and Gunnar Bengtsson/Sven Zetterberg were second and third, respectively, with Bengt Jonsson/Sölve Relve seventh overall. A month later Carl-Magnus Skogh came third in the Swedish Rally — an event in which overall victory was to elude SAAB for some time to come.

Whilst Skogh, Carlsson and Harald Kronegård competed in home events, Rolf Mellde took on the *Tour d'Europe*, partnered by Swedish motoring journalist Sverker Benson. Organized from Germany, the event started in Hanover and then went south to Reims, Lisbon, Madrid, Monte Carlo, Rome, Trieste, Dubrovnik, Athens and Istanbul before heading north again for Hanover. A distance of 8,125 miles in 13 days.

Unfortunately, the rules of the event (sponsored by Continental tyres) were rather ambiguous, stating that the route between the controls was free — except that there would be secret controls along the route! Mellde was assured at the drivers' briefing that this was not the case, and he left Hanover with the other 64 entrants.

The Swedes hit trouble in Reims when they lost four hours repairing the carburettor, and then headed south for Lisbon. Once through the Spanish border, Benson took over to allow Mellde to rest and promptly missed a junction, sending them off the route. He rectified his error and headed towards Lisbon via Miranda, which they approached from the south, but on arriving at Lisbon they were told that there had been a secret control on the north side of Miranda. All would have been lost had not Mellde kept a petrol receipt from the garage in Miranda where they had tanked-up the Saab; it was this receipt which persuaded the organizers, headed by a Mr Tietsch, to let the Swedes carry on without any penalties. The next stop was Trieste, a journey at an average speed of 62 mph, so not surprisingly only 36 cars made the Adriatic port without penalties.

From there to Istanbul, the rallying — and the cheating — really started. The next control was hidden in Dubrovnik and only a select few drivers were told of its existence, but not the Swedes. Despite a thorough search Mellde and Benson couldn't find the control, so Mellde fell back on his old trick of keeping the petrol receipt. Driving in two-hour shifts towards the Greek border, tiredness and dust began to take its toll. At one point both fell asleep and they had lost four hours by the time they reached the Greek border. Despite an

Always a gentleman! Erik Carlsson salutes a young supporter after the Norwegian Viking Rally in 1956.

exchange of heated words, all was forgotten when they discovered that none of the other competitors had reached the border. They were leading! Despite their tiredness and the lost hours Mellde calculated that if they averaged 55 mph (the official average speed was a paltry 31 mph) they would reach Athens without penalties. 'I don't think I have ever scared so many dogs and chickens in my entire life as I did that night,' Mellde recalls. But make it they did, the gods obviously being on SAAB's side that time, and on reaching Athens the exhausted duo had eight hours of much needed sleep before heading off to Istanbul, where they had a doctor standing by to treat their tired eyes.

The trip north, via Belgrade and Vienna, was comparatively easy apart from hitting an oil patch left on the road by a wrecked oil tanker, when fortunately, Mellde managed to keep the Saab on the road.

Rather than risk getting lost Mellde and Benson did an extra 93 miles on the autobahn before reaching Hanover — the only car to do so without incurring penalty points — and victory was theirs. Or was it? Suddenly there were 50 penalty points for having missed a non-existent secret control. So exhausted were they after the event, the pair didn't even bother to argue, and so they lost first place to the Ford Taunus of Edwin von Regius and Joachim Springer. As an aside, that car was shod with Continental tyres, whereas the Saab was on Goodyears. . . . Mellde and Benson had driven 8,383 miles, and changed three sets of tyres and brake shoes, while the rally had also taken its toll of the crew, Mellde and Benson having lost eight and six kilos, respectively.

Revenge is sweet, though, and the *Tour d'Europe* had barely finished when Bengt Jonsson and Kjell Persson won the Wiesbaden Rally in their Saab 93 on June 24, 1956, a doubly sweet victory in that it was the marque's first international win.

Later that year Saabs dominated Norway's Viking Rally, Carl-Magnus Skogh winning, followed by Erik Carlsson, and with Ivar Andersson fourth overall. The classic Scandia Trophy was shared by Erik and Carl-Magnus that year, said to be the one and only time they ever shared anything. Despite these victories the Swedish Championship was once again won by a Volkswagen driver, though both Erik and Carl-Magnus were by now threatening VW's supremacy. Further down the results list a new generation of navigators and drivers was beginning to appear and Bo Reinicke took third place in the Junior class for navigators; in the sixties Bo was to navigate both Stig Blomqvist and Per Eklund and come out of retirement for the 1979 RAC Rally to navigate Ola Strömberg. Around this time Carl Orrenius, soon to become a Saab regular, turned up at his first rally complete

Erik Carlsson gained his nickname 'Carlsson På Taket' (Carlsson-on-the-roof) early in his career and immediately put it on the door of his rally car.

with white collar, tie and hat.

With an eye on exports, and particularly the USA, the SAAB sales department decided that if it was possible to sell European sports cars to the Americans it would also be possible to sell Saabs. Initially, 200 Saab 93s were shipped to Connecticut, where they were enthusiastically received, but sales would have to be on a grander scale if a profit was to be made.

Rather optimistically, SAAB entered Mellde and Greta Molander in the Sebring 12-Hours race, but it was decided (wisely) not to follow the plan. Instead, they entered a team of cars into the Great American Mountain Rally (a 1,500-mile event run at an average speed of 43 mph). However, the then managing director, Ragnar Wahlgren, turned the idea down several times before he allowed Mellde to prepare and ship three engines and gearboxes to the United States, and with the customs being particularly awkward the cars were only ready the day before the event started.

Mellde was partnered by the American, Morrow Mushkin, while the two other cars had all-American crews — Bob Wehman/Louis Braun and Gerald and Doris Lankowitz. Mushkin was

rather apprehensive about whether the car would last the event following Mellde's two days of practice, but nevertheless he turned up at the start. Interpreting meanings of words was the first problem Mellde and Mushkin encountered when, on the first stage, they came to a T-junction. 'Left?' asked Mellde.

'Right', replied a confident Mushkin, with which Mellde promptly turned left — 10 minutes later they realised they were heading in the wrong direction.

At the first rest halt they were lying 50th overall, not a very auspicious debut. By the restart the next morning there had been a snowfall, making the road too slippery for many of the competitors to drive up the steeper hills — except Mellde, that is, who reversed up-hill in a series of zig-zags elevating them to sixth overall, where they finished. More importantly, Wehman/Braun won the event and the Lankowitzs finished 17th, giving SAAB the manufacturer's team prize plus first, second and third in class.

SAAB's American business could not have got off to a better start, and 1956 could not have had a better ending.

Chapter 4

Harald's five tough months

Right from the start, the factory-entered Saabs have always been accompanied by private entrants trying to emulate the works drivers. One such driver was Harald Kronegård, who was later to achieve rather more fame on race tracks than on rally routes. Like many drivers, Harald tried several marques before meeting a couple of Saab drivers who were connected with Gunnar V. Philipson. This contact led to Kronegård purchasing a T-car, one that had been taken off the production line before it had received any heavy insulation material.

Harald prepared the car with the aid of some of Philipson's mechanics, and because of the close factory connection bought what few spare parts he required at a discount. 'Not that the car needed much. The Saab was tougher than most cars. The only thing I can remember that needed frequent attention was the exhaust manifold, which cracked and had to be changed every so often. It sounded like hell when it was broken!' recalls Harald.

As with most privateers, Harald was more interested in making the finish line rather than going flat-out for victory, and consequently he didn't get many championship points. Some years, however, were better than others, and 1957 is one that Harald remembers particularly well. . . .

'I entered the Tulip Rally in the April with my own car. The result was nothing to be proud of — we came sixth in class and 61st overall. My co-driver, Jan Carlqvist, took the car back to Sweden while I flew to Italy to do the Mille Miglia with Charlie Lohmander in his car.'

(The Mille Miglia was a 1,000-mile race, run on open roads. From the start in Brescia it went east to Padua, then south to Pescara, over the mountains to Rome, north to Florence, then on to Bologna and back to Brescia. The event was banned in 1957 following a horrifying accident when the Marquis de Portago and his co-driver, Edward Nelson, left the road in their Ferrari, killing themselves and 11 spectators.)

'Charlie Lohmander came directly from the Acropolis Rally in Greece, where his wife had been his co-driver. They withdrew from that event, but a Frenchman called Henri Blanchoud drove his Saab into second place behind a Ferrari 250GT.

'We had two days to get the car ready before the start, and we were the only Scandinavians out of 25 starters in the 750 cc class, although Olle Persson had entered a Porsche in a bigger class.

'The event itself was without drama. I drove most of the time as Charlie was a bit too careful on an event like the Mille Miglia, which he admitted. While the car ran perfectly, petrol was available at the controls and the Pirelli tyres were extremely strong — we didn't have to change a single tyre.

'The worst problem was visibility, especially rearwards. Rear vision was vital as the organizers had started the smallest cars first and the fastest cars last. Also, we had taped the rear window over so there was only a small gap to see the lights of the rapidly approaching Ferraris and Maseratis. By the end of the event I was driving with one eye on the rear mirror all the time. The other problem was the turbulence created as the fast cars roared past; you really had to grip the steering wheel to stop the car being buffeted off the road!

'We won the class, probably because we were used to high speeds over Sweden's rough terrain. We were even given some small prizes — plus the honour — but no money.

'I had barely set foot in Sweden when I received a telephone call from SAAB summoning me to

Swedish amateur Harald Kronegard being guided by Charlie Lohmander on the 1957 Mille Miglia and, below, in Casablanca the following month celebrating second place on the Atlas-Oasis Rally.

lot — a free trip for myself and my wife, food and some money!

'On arrival in Morocco we had a grand reception with flowers, the whole works. They really were quite impressed in having a driver come all the way from Sweden.

'My co-driver was Leonce Beysson. Half-French and half-Moroccan, Leonce was a truck-driver by trade and had done the rally before so he was well used to the desert.

'The start of the rally was accompanied by a most impressive ceremony, and we headed off to Casablanca. We had barely got there before a throttle linkage jumped off, but we managed to fix it with a piece of wire.

'We arrived at the first control with plenty of time in hand, only to be told that we had missed a passage control. We knew we hadn't, but the organizers wanted a Peugeot to win. . . . However,

Harald back in Sweden just before he crashed on the first stage, and below, in the loaned African car on the Thousand Lakes, in Finland, when he again rolled heavily, though went on to finish seventh.

Trollhättan. They told me that they had shipped a car to Morocco for the Rallye Atlas-Oasis, which started in Rabat and finished in Casablanca. None of the works drivers could do it, so did I want to? SAAB's dealer in Morocco was paying for the

'The Sahara was something quite new for me, but I enjoyed every mile of it!'

there was still a long way to go and the roads gradually deteriorated. Loose stones were causing a lot of problems, but we had an extra windscreen of plexiglass outside the original one and that helped.

'In the middle of the desert the engine started to boil and we topped it up with mineral water. Then we encountered water problems of a different type — we had to ford a river. Many of the drivers were too keen to get across and quickly flooded their engines, but I took it very cautiously as the water was halfway up the doors, while Leonce walked in front of the car. We were out to finish and the locals were very impressed by the little Saab's performance.

'Towards the end of the event it was clear that we were going to win, and we were escorted through all the towns towards the finish in Casablanca. Eventually we were classified second overall, behind a Peugeot that had missed one of the passage controls! Fortunately the Swedish consul was there to calm me down, so I accepted their trophy and money, while Leonce was more than happy to have the car's Speedpilot.

'On returning to Sweden my own car was ready for the Swedish Rally. Having been abroad for

quite a bit I wanted to show-off to everyone at home. Consequently I went off the road on the first stage and bent the car quite badly. Somehow we got it back on to the road to finish the stage. Somewhat chastened, I was more careful after that and eventually finished tenth.

'By the end of the Swedish Rally the Moroccan car had returned and I borrowed it for the Thousand Lakes. There was still a lot of Moroccan sand in it when Mario Pavoni and I started from Jyväskylä! Again, I was going quite fast until I rolled it; eventually we got the car back on to the road, but it was so steep that it rolled back into the ditch and then a further 30 metres down the slope. Our only solution was to continue rolling the car down the slope to another road, which is what we did. It took us a long time, and we were penalized for damaged bodywork, even though we spent the rest of the rally trying to reshape the car with wooden poles at service halts. Eventually we were classified seventh.'

Remember, Harald Kronegård was an amateur, but still he managed to compete in five international rallies in as many months, plus a host of home events.

Harald Kronegård on his way to sixth in class on the 1957 Tulip Rally.

The class-winning Saab of Kronegård and Lohmander arrives at the finish point after a gruelling stage on the 1957 Mille Miglia.

Chapter 5

Lots of medals — in racing

Erik Carlsson is regarded as one of the greatest rally drivers, although it is impossible to say if he is the greatest of all, simply because there is no proof. Erik never won any championships while rallying, although he came close to winning the European Championship in 1959, when he lost by one point to Paul Coltelloni in his Citroen. Even so, Erik has four championship medals at home, two each from tarmac and ice-racing. Funnily enough the old two-stroke was a very competitive racer in those days. Although the factory never entered two-cylinder 92s in racing, plenty of enthusiasts such as Gösta Bergqvist and Harald Kronegård did. The main reason for the lack of works-entered cars was simply that there was no championship to fight for.

During the winter months motor clubs would plough circuits on frozen lakes and fields where they could hold events at short notice, assured of an enthusiastic audience. But the winters were not to be trusted, and nobody dared to organize a complete series of events as the organizers often had to cancel them at the last minute. Summertime was not much better, as only the Karslskoga Motorclub possessed a permanent circuit, at Gelleråsen, which was later to become the mecca for Swedish racing fans.

By 1958, however, there was enough interest shown for a Swedish ice-racing championship to be inaugurated. In the same year, SAAB introduced the 93B with a new one-piece windscreen and blinker-type indicators. There was also the 750GT (mainly for the United States) with a higher compression ratio and a power output of 45 bhp.

The first ice-racing championship fell to Erik Carlsson, although it was no easy victory as he was competing against DKWs in the same class. In particular, there was one driven by Sigurd Isacson,

and not a single race passed without some incident between Erik and Sigurd — not all of them legal, either!

1959 was the same. The final qualifier was run in northern Vilhelmina, on March 22, following which Erik had sufficient points to clinch the championship. But Isacson protested and it was not until May 25 that Erik finally got confirmation of the championship, by which time everyone had forgotten about it. Carl-Magnus Skogh and Hans Hagbäck, both driving Saabs, were third and fourth, respectively.

Racing 'special standard' cars, the engines were tuned to produce about 50 bhp, while the cars had 100 kilos pared off them. Even so, Erik maintains that the Saabs were 'nothing' compared with Isacson's 'German cycle'.

SAAB had a firm grip on the 850 cc class, which they didn't relinquish until the introduction of the Fiat Abarth 1000 in 1966. Following the success of the ice-racing championship, one for tarmac racing was introduced in 1959, and just to show that SAAB's dominance in ice-racing was no fluke, Erik won the tarmac title in both 1959 and 1960.

1959 was to prove a good year for SAAB's racing activities. Sten Bielke travelled thoughout Europe winning races in Italy and France, and two in Austria, where he became champion. However, the support from SAAB and Gunnar V. Philipson was insufficient, and he quit at the end of the season. That same year a 12-hours race was organized at the Skarpnäck airfield circuit near Stockholm. It was for pure standard cars, and the organizers managed to get most dealers to enter a car. SAAB's entry was driven by Rolf Mellde and Carl-Magnus Skogh, who eventually won their class after beating the DKWs. Undaunted, the

Although Erik Carlsson never won a Swedish Championship in rallying he took four titles in racing, two of them on ice.

Germans returned the following year to win handsomely. The best SAAB could do this time was sixth and seventh in class, despite protesting the DKWs. (Apparently the Trollhättan cars were too legal, for a local notary had selected two cars from the production line to ensure that they were completely standard.) By 1961 though, things were back to normal with SAAB getting a one-two victory, while 1962 was even better with Saabs filling the top three places, Carl Orrenius coming in third, despite rolling his car.

In most normal races Saabs were unbeatable except for the two years when Sigurd Isacson was ice-racing champion in 1960 and 1961. SAAB's star drivers were Erik Berger, Gösta Karlsson, Bo Johansson (later renamed Brasta after his home town) and Sigvard Johansson (one of the Competition Department's ace mechanics), who won almost every race they entered.

The Group 2 cars were run in the 850 cc class, while the Group 3 limit was 1,000 cc. The main opposition in Group 3 came from pure sports cars, but the regulations allowed the Saab to be tuned to 60 bhp, and the use of aluminium body parts reduced the cars' weight considerably.

Motor sport was still run from within the technical department, but in 1962 Bosse Hellberg was employed as SAAB's first full-time Competitions Manager.

To win national championships is one thing, but to win the European Championship is quite different. In the two years that SAAB were racing seriously it was called the European Cup for standard cars, and that was SAAB's ultimate goal.

During the Cup's first year, 1963, Björn Rothstein, Gösta Karlsson and Tom Trana (in the Volvo 544) joined forces all over Europe, but their efforts received little attention back home in Sweden.

Racing was simple in those days. The drivers used their racing cars as transport between the circuits, carrying the racing engine in the boot and

The battles between the Saabs and the DKWs were highlights of racing in Sweden in the fifties.

28

The 12-hour races at the Skarpnäck airfield circuit proved to be very popular events in 1959 and 1960. Here we see some of the action at the Le Mans-type start, during driver changes and out on the track.

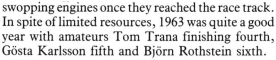

swopping engines once they reached the race track. In spite of limited resources, 1963 was quite a good year with amateurs Tom Trana finishing fourth, Gösta Karlsson fifth and Björn Rothstein sixth.

Points were calculated in a rather complicated fashion and despite there being several classes there was only one overall champion.

The following year Björn Rothstein decided to do it professionally with a Saab, and with only two rounds of the Cup to go Björn stood a good chance of winning outright. All he had to do was ensure that the second driver in his class was as far behind him as possible (the overall win in each event was awarded to the driver who had beaten his class

29

Long-distance races can be won on the track but lost at the pits. Here is some slick work by mechanics of the SAAB team during a stop for replacement front tyres.

opponents by the biggest margin).

Rothstein's closest rivals were Warwick Banks in a 1,000 cc Mini and Sir John Whitmore in the 1,600 cc Cortina. Normally these drivers had greater difficulty in maintaining the gap between themselves and their rivals than Björn did with the opposition in his class. However, at the penultimate round in Budapest, Hungary, there were insufficient starters in Björn's class, so Bosse Hellberg entered his private Saab, fitted with a racing engine, in the race. It was all something of a joke as Rothstein roared off into a class lead with the other SAAB drivers doing just enough to complete the necessary 80 per cent of Björn's laps. After four laps, Hellberg, Gösta Karlsson and Bosse Johansson headed for the pits where they washed their cars, while Johansson even stopped on the track to spend a penny behind a tree . . . All they had to do was finish the six-hour race. By the finish, though, the lap counting had become so confused that Gösta Karlsson had to stop 100 yards before the

finishing line and wait. The tactic worked, all the Saabs got their 80 per cent in time and Björn scored his vital points. Consequently, the results list looked rather strange as second place went to an unknown Dutch driver, Koster, and third to an equally unknown Hungarian, Hollos.

But the European Cup was not at Trollhättan yet as there was still one race in Italy to do. The SAAB plan was to ensure that neither Banks nor Whitmore won their respective classes by too big a margin.

Consequently, SAAB paid the entry fee, travel to the event and expenses for a couple of fast Swedish drivers: Jan-Erik Andreasson in a Mini and Svante Vorrsjö in a Cortina. Their job was to keep in touch with the English drivers while Rothstein fought off his opposition. During practice it looked as though SAAB's devious plan would work, the two Swedes beating the opposition fair and square. But the best laid plans of mice and men . . . During the race both Swedes were plagued with engine

Racing was an important form of competition for Saabs in the sixties and the surfaces varied from tarmac to ice and gravel. There was also a variety of opposition, from DKWs and Ford Anglias to Porsches.

Sigge Johansson is a mastermind when it comes to tuning Saabs, and in 1969 he raced his own supercharged 1,420 cc V4, which produced 182 bhp.

problems while Rothstein drove faster than ever. (The Saab had a top speed of 115 mph yet his race average was nearly 90 mph!) Banks went on to win the European Cup and SAAB came away having learnt a strict lesson on rule-bending.

SAAB's interest in racing waned in the mid-sixties with the introduction of the Fiat Abarth in Group 2 and the Cortina Lotuses in Group 3. Nevertheless, the little two-strokes won seven ice-racing and nine tarmac-racing championships, a record still unequalled in Sweden by any other manufacturer.

Across the Atlantic, in America, the 99 model has proved to be one of the fastest cars in the Showroom Stock class. As with Swedish production saloon racing the cars and tyres must be absolutely standard. Nevertheless, sometimes rules can still be bent, for example 'soot' can be sprayed into the combustion chambers to raise the compression ratio and, of course, the cars can be lightened. To achieve the correct weight at scrutineering it has been known for some cars to have the sills filled with ice, which, of course, melts before the race.

Yet despite rule-bending by others the (legal) Saabs have done well in this class. Stig Blomqvist led the SAAB team to victory in a guest appearance at Lime Rock in 1976, following which Saabs have won just about everything they've entered. In 1978 and 1979 Don Knowles (Washington) was National Champion in Showroom Stock B class, closely followed by more Saabs, while in 1979, Ron Christensen won the Showroom Stock A class in his 99 Turbo.

But standard is standard, and no four-stroke engine can come close to the sound of a fully tuned two-stroke. The kick you got when you heard 25 96s coming down the straight at Karlskoga race track was incredible. The hysterical noise from those straight exhausts and of metal meeting metal in the first corner are now, unfortunately, just sweet memories.

32

Björn Rothstein came very close to winning the European Championship in 1964.

Fifteen years of progress depicted by two Saab Turbos which dominated Showroom Stock racing in the United States in 1979.

33

Chapter 6

The Saab Sonett — so neat

Lack of power has always been a problem with Saabs in competition; it wasn't really until the debut of the 99 Turbo in 1978 that they could match their competitors.

When the Saab 92s were beaten by the Porsche-engined VWs it was due to lack of horsepower. The 93 was better with some 60 bhp, but that still wasn't enough to compensate for the car's immense strength, strength born out of heavy metal.

If SAAB were to have a real chance of reaching the top in international events they had to produce a lightweight GT car. One already existed on Rolf Mellde's drawing board, and Mellde had it all worked out when he was given the go-ahead for the Saab Sonett in 1956.

The basis of the car was the Saab 93, with the 748 cc engine tuned to 57 bhp at 5,000 rpm, the equivalent of 76.9 bhp per litre — an incredible figure at that time. Mellde and his engineers, Lars-Olof Olsson, Olle Lindqvist and Gösta Svensson, reached that figure by raising the compression ratio from 7.2:1 to 10:1. A twin-choke carburettor fed the three cylinders via an intake manifold that looked like a refugee from a Hoover factory.

In all, six Sonetts were hand-built, the first two with SAAB's original three-speed gearbox and the others with a new four-speed unit developed in Trollhättan.

The aluminium semi-monocoque chassis was built up from a series of boxes with the drive-train mounted backwards to lower the car's centre of gravity. The three-section glass-fibre bodyshell was designed by Sixten Sason (SAAB's chief designer until his death in 1967), and despite the heavy glass-fibre bodyshell the Sonett still weighed in at under 500 kilos. An all-aluminium body would have lowered the weight still further, but it would have been too fragile.

As the Sonett was primarily designed for competition little consideration was given to the creature comforts of either the driver or the co-driver, but the driver was kept busy with a full instrument display that also included a temperature gauge for the gearbox oil.

Two-stroke engines are most efficient when they run cold, the Sonett's operating best at 50 degrees C. To achieve a continuously low operating temperature water was fed to the cooling system by twin pumps regulated by thermostats, the hot water simply being expelled into the air. The ignition timing was also adjustable from the cockpit as extremely hard surface-gap spark plugs were used, which, together with the engine's extreme port timing, made the Sonett rather difficult to start. Also, the engine had to be kept above 3,000 rpm, otherwise the plugs would oil-up.

All this added up to a very quick motor car. Mellde and his colleagues achieved the following times when testing the car, the highest top speed being attained when a hardtop and different gearing was fitted: 0-50 mph, 8 secs; 0-62 mph, 12 secs; standing quarter-mile, 18 secs; standing kilometre, 34 secs; top speed, 112-133 mph.

Rolf Mellde gave the Sonett its debut in August 1957, at Karlskoga, where he won, followed by Harald Kronegard and Clas Bäckström. Mellde's car weighed in at 696 kilos and with a 59 bhp engine it was more than a match for the opposition.

The cars were then raced at various trotting tracks throughout Sweden, but on September 15, 1957, the Sonett had what turned out to be its last

The Saab Sonett appeared in a few
races in 1957, but only six examples
of the original model were built.

race, the legendary Erik Lundgren taking it to victory at the Solvalla trotting track, just outside Stockholm. The small two-seater could have grown into a truly competitive car, but it never got the chance. When it was ready to race, the rules were changed overnight, and so the Sonett was obsolete. Group 3 was introduced, and that heralded the lightweight 93, powered by a Sonett engine.

Mellde's Sonett grew old overnight and he was never again permitted to use the car for competition himself as the factory considered it too dangerous for a man in his position — head of the Technical Department.

One of the early Sonetts being chased by a Lotus Eleven. Note the crowd of people at the track edge and the lack of any barrier!

Chapter 7

The toughest ever

Erik Carlsson won numerous events during his outstanding 15-years rally career, more than he can remember, in fact. RAC Rally three times, Monte Carlo twice, the Swedish once — the list goes on.

But he regards his best achievements as two seconds on the *Marathon de la Route*, better known as the Spa-Sofia-Liège. It was on these events that Erik's phenomenal ability to get the most out of himself and the car reached its peak, for it was his and his co-driver Gunnar Palm's physical and mental toughness that paid off. 'It was Erik's absolutely best results, no doubt,' says Gunnar Palm.

Erik took part in the event six times, from 1959 to 1964, but the first four times he was out of luck. One year a piston broke, another year it was the rotor arm that stopped him. Originally the rally was called the Marathon and it started in the Liège suburb of Spa, and then headed for Rome, where it turned back. Later, the turning point, with an hour's rest, was to become Sofia, in Bulgaria.

During the 3,479 miles event, the route took the drivers over some of the worst Alpine roads including the Passo di Gavia, Passo di Cruche Domino and the Passo de Stelvio. The organizers couldn't have devised simpler rules if they had tried. All the competitors had to ensure was that they entered the controls from the right direction within their permitted time. Between the controls the route was free. The organizers didn't arrange petrol halts, or anything, while the average speeds were quite ridiculous — 143 miles in 1 hour 40 minutes. 'Impossible,' protested the co-driver. 'Is that so?', replied the organizers, not taking a blind bit of notice.

The rules were strict as well. If a competitor was one minute late at Sofia, the organizers kept his time card and road-book with a 'Sorry, see you next year?'. But they were true sportsmen as well. In the late-fifties, Sunbeam protested against a minor detail on the Saab and the following year their entry was refused!

During the 1963 event, Gunnar Palm only drove 250 of the 3,479 miles, Erik Carlsson doing the rest. And how he did it! The opposition was spearheaded by Eugen Böhringer in a two-seater Mercedes-Benz 230 SL. The handicapping system favoured the larger cars, so Erik had to drive flat-out on the twisty sections to make up time lost to the bigger cars on the fast ones. Co-driver Palm's job was easy since nobody had the opportunity to be early at a control.

Yugoslavia's and Bulgaria's roads took their toll of the cars. If it rained the roads became a quagmire, and without the rain it was choking dust. Shock absorbers would get so hot that paint would flake off and the wings would be perforated from the inside by the continous bombardment of stones. Then there was the everyday traffic, as the roads weren't closed off to the public during the rally.

A SAAB mechanic was sent to the Albanian border to refuel Erik's car. Unfortunately he worked on the assumption that you could buy fuel at the border, but you couldn't. On the verge of jumping into the Adriatic rather than facing Erik's wrath, he was saved by some British competitors who gave him petrol.

As they approached the Austrian border on the return from Sofia, a fatigued Gunnar Palm started seeing green men! 'Keep going,' he told Erik, 'don't take any notice.' Fortunately, Erik did take notice — those little green men turned out to be Austrian customs officers!

This little episode made them realise that they

The Spa-Sofia-Liège involved 5,600 kilometres of virtually non-stop motoring, and Erik Carlsson and Gunnar Palm finished second twice. 'My best achievement ever', says Erik.

The Marathon de la Route was the name given to the Spa-Sofia-Liège, and it took competitors through some of the roughest roads existing over a large part of Europe. Success on this event was always a major achievement for even the most talented of competition drivers.

were over-tired and, aware that the next stage was fairly easy, they settled down for an hour's nap. Gunnar set his alarm, but they both slept through it. This time it was Eugen Eger, Mercedes' chief mechanic and one of Fangio's old mechanics, who tapped Erik on the shoulder and got them on their way.

It was the same year that Rauno Aaltonen, driving one of the big Healeys, left the road while leading. The 'ditch' he landed in was some 800 metres deep and the big Healey nearly dropped off the edge of the cliff. Fortunately, co-driver Tony Ambrose managed to clamber out of the car and with the aid of some locals secured it. The Spa-Sofia-Liège legend is full of such stories.

Rauno Aaltonen won the following year, 1964, with Erik once again second, although not without his problems. It all started before the event with Gunnar Palm's recce. Following their second place in the Polish Rally, Gunnar headed off to Yugoslavia to start the recce, stopping off in Vienna for a couple of days' rest. Wandering around a bookshop he found some maps of Yugoslavia, which he was convinced none of the other competitors would have.

The recce was then delayed when Gunnar was in an accident with a lorry on a narrow mountain road. Gunnar's car was too badly damaged to drive, and with his face badly cut and bleeding he struggled to the nearest village where he managed to get patched up. From there he hitched a lift on a lorry to the nearest town from where he could get the damaged car looked after.

He then called the Swedish embassy in Belgrade and arranged an air-ticket back to Sweden. Hitch-hiking again he made it to Rijeka where he persuaded the captain of an old DC3 freight-plane

to fly him to Belgrade. From there he arranged for the damaged car to be sent back to Sweden before flying home himself.

When he finally got back to Gothenburg he was taken immediately to Trollhättan, where he picked up a new car. That same night, he and Liz Nyström — Pat Moss-Carlsson's co-driver — drove non-stop back down to Yugoslavia to complete the recce. It was all worth it, for Gunnar's new maps revealed some useful farm tracks which shortened the route considerably.

On arriving at this short-cut during the rally, Erik wasn't too happy. 'Damn you, Gunnar, if this doesn't work.' But Erik was getting fed-up with being stuck behind a works Citroên and reluctantly took Gunnar's route.

The little Saab bounced and banged its way over the fields and through the woods before getting back to the main road — just behind a factory Citroên! Erik nearly exploded as it was some 6¼ miles to the next control with no passing places. Fortunately, Gunnar's reputation was saved when, on arriving at the control, they found it was a different Citroên and they had, in fact, saved ten minutes. Erik was pleased. 'Gunnar was very good at these things,' he recalls.

Albania's border must have a jinx on Erik and Gunnar for it was nearly their downfall in 1964 as well. Waiting at the border with full petrol cans was Bosse Hellberg and a Swedish journalist who helped the team out. In a quick stop Gunnar unloaded their empty fuel cans and the journalist replaced them. Unfortunately they were the wrong ones and they were empty, as Erik and Gunnar found out when the car ran to a halt about six miles before the next control/fuel stop. The only liquid Gunnar could find was four bottles of alcohol used to stop the carburettors from icing up. With nothing to lose, Gunnar emptied the alcohol into the petrol tank and crossed his fingers. They reached the next control. You have to be lucky sometimes!

Of the 98 cars that started only 21 finished and the other Swedish entries were out of luck. Berndt Jansson crashed his VW Beetle into a bridge, Bo Ljungfeldt went off when his Ford Mustang's lights failed and Gunnar Blomqvist (no relation to Stig) had to withdraw because of gearbox problems. Rune Larsson also suffered gearbox problems in his VW, but his co-driver managed to make a hole in the rear floor and changed gear with a spanner, while Henny-Britt Ehringe, at the time Sweden's leading lady driver, went off the road and broke her leg.

Erik and Gunnar started at 10 pm on the Tuesday and finished at 7.00 pm on the Saturday in covering the 3,479 miles, while during the one-hour stop in Sofia they managed to change shock absorbers. But it wasn't enough, and Erik still finished second behind Aaltonen, with Pat Moss-Carlsson fourth. Nevertheless, it was a worthy effort by the SAAB team.

Carlsson and Palm hurry through a pedestrian-lined street with Saab number 52, and have time for an exchange of views at a control point in the middle of the night.

Chapter 8

A Saab at Le Mans

A Saab 93B in the Le Mans 24-Hours sounds crazy today, but back in 1959 it was an expression of the absolute faith many drivers had in the little two-strokes.

The enthusiast behind the venture was Sture Nottorp, who had entered his Frazer Nash at Le Mans back in 1954. This time he wanted to enter a Saab, so he consulted Rolfe Mellde, who took it upon himself to get the car prepared for the 750 cc class. Nottorp was backed by two friends who had helped him on his previous Le Mans effort. Rune Berthilsson, formerly head of the Swedish Ferrari team, but now working for SAAB, also joined the party. He in turn organized the pit crew and also brought along one of Sweden's top racing drivers, Gunnar Bengtsson.

Mellde had the car completely stripped down and everything that wasn't necessary was thrown out and a 21.5-gallon fuel tank installed. On the engine side, Mellde polished the overflow, raised the compression ratio to 10:1 and fitted three huge Solex carburettors. This resulted in 65 bhp at 6,700 rpm to power the 723 kilo Saab.

A four-speed gearbox was being experimented with at the time, and the Le Mans project was an ideal test-bed for it; without a four-speed unit the little Saab wouldn't have stood a chance. Car, spares and anything else that might be needed were put into a rented lorry and the team headed off for Le Mans, and after some trouble they eventually reached the Sarthe circuit at 5.30 am, only 4½ hours before scrutineering.

Fortunately, scrutineering didn't present any problems; leather bonnet straps and mud flaps were fitted and their starting number was changed from 42 to 44. Nobody really paid any attention to the Saab, apart from one scrutineer who wondered

'whether it was suitable for this job'.

A great deal of attention was paid to the car's preparation, and everything was checked and double-checked. Engine, brakes, steering, oil, water, throttle linkages, tyre pressure, driveshafts (the left one had leaked a little during practice), the gearbox (it was a little stiff changing down to second), lights, fuel consumption. The list was endless.

Extra attention was paid to the rear of the car. Reflecting tape was stuck to the back of the body as after all the Saab only had a top speed of 105 mph compared to the fastest cars' 180 mph. Even the brake adjusters were painted white so they would be seen at night, the driver's seat was adjusted and the distributor changed because it had a few hairline cracks in it. Nothing was forgotten. Then they polished the car, recalls Berthilsson.

On Saturday, June 20, 1959, at 4.00 pm Nottorp sprinted across the track to start his first stint behind the wheel. After a few yards the car sputtered to a halt; he had forgotten to switch on the electrical fuel pump! But as Berthilsson pointed out in his report, '10 metres don't matter that much in a 24-hours race'. After 3 hrs 12 mins and 32 laps, Nottorp came into the pits for the first scheduled stop, and having refuelled and checked the water Gunnar Bengtsson took over. He pitted again at 10.34 pm, and in 3 mins 37 secs the Saab was refuelled, the spark plugs renewed and the tyres checked — in 64 laps they had lost just half a millimetre.

The third stop came at 0.59 am, when the team introduced a new phrase to the Saab Competitions Department, 'Massaging the drive joints'. Two mechanics lay under the car and massaged the joints to get the grease back into them! At the same

A Saab at Le Mans may have looked somewhat incongruous alongside the purpose-built endurance racing cars, but in 1959 this carefully prepared and well-driven car finished 12th overall, a most creditable performance.

time the brakes were being adjusted and the car refuelled. Just before he left the pits Nottorp was told that the British-entered 750GT driven by Hurrell had withdrawn due to a seized piston.

A broken alternator bracket made the fourth pit stop at 5.20 am a bit longer at 7 mins 15 secs, during which they also checked the breaker points and massaged the joints again. Then, after three pit stops and 232 laps the little Saab crossed the finishing line, 12th out of 13 finishers from 55 starters.

During the 24 hours the car averaged 81 mph on a 4 per cent petroil mix, while the brake linings had worn only one millimetre. As an insurance the engineers had fitted a windscreen washer jet on each of the four brake drums to cool the brakes. These could be activated by simply pressing a pump mounted on a reservoir next to the driver's seat (that was 18 years before Broadspeed tried it on the group 2 Jaguar). The device was never used because Le Mans' long straights allowed the brakes to cool down. The light blue Le Mans Saab was driven later in the year by Erik Carlsson at the Falkenburg round of the Swedish Championship, but that wasn't as interesting as the Le Mans story.

Chapter 9

Safari — the missing victory

When Erik Carlsson won the RAC Rally in 1961 one of his prizes was a ticket to and from Nairobi for the East African Safari Rally; it was one of the organizers' ways of getting people to compete in their event. Then, in January 1962, Erik won the Monte Carlo Rally and another ticket from the organizers of the East African Safari. It was obvious that he should make use of these tickets! His second ticket was given to Pat Moss-Carlsson, who had a brand new, unprepared car shipped to Nairobi for her by SAAB.

The organizers had arranged for Erik to have a Kenyan dentist as his co-driver. He had done all the Safaris and had been in the winning team one year so he was well experienced. Erik took him out for a test run. 'He nearly died' says Erik. 'It was a wide road and you could jump and do whatever you liked. He was completely silent when we returned home.'

The dentist's wife didn't think that Erik's driving was considerate enough, so the day after the test drive the dentist 'phoned Erik. 'Sorry, but . . .' His place was taken by a SAAB technician, Karl-Erik 'the Beard' Svensson.

'We could have won easily,' Erik remembers 'but we quite simply drove too fast. Finally the car was beyond repair. Literally, everything was worn out, the bottom was gone, brake pipes torn apart — everything.'

Driving in East Africa is not the same as driving in Europe, that was SAAB's and Erik's lesson. Nevertheless, Erik still finished sixth and Pat, in her standard car, was third.

SAAB realised they had a chance of winning and came back the following year. Erik wasn't to win that year, either, but SAAB were to get a lot of publicity.

Erik went down to East Africa full of confidence after his second Monte win and with his then new co-driver, Gunnar Palm. The Safari was just what they wanted. Gunnar Palm: 'It was in Africa that we realised how well we worked together. The worse things got the harder we tried — both of us. We are different in many ways, but stubborn in the same way.' After the first loop Carlsson and Palm were in the lead. In fact some of the times they set 17 years ago are still to be beaten! The timing wasn't of the highest quality with rather slack marshalling, of which the crafty Swedes took full advantage!

The second loop took the drivers down into Tanzania, and after Mbulu they were still in the lead. Then the rally took them through plains of tall grass where they hit trouble, literally. They were doing about 62 mph when an animal ran straight out in front of the car. It was impossible to avoid it and after the impact the creature was thrown in front of the car before the Saab ran over it. They continued for about 100 metres before stopping and, with the aid of the roof-mounted searchlight, tried to see if the mysterious animal was moving. It wasn't.

Using the jack, they managed to straighten-out the front bumper that was fouling the wheel. Once they got going again they heard a noise from the left front wheel and made the classic error of not stopping to check. It was important to be first on the road because of the dust, especially at night. The roads were deteriorating all the time and the battered car was suffering heavily. Suddenly it stopped, although the engine was still running. Between them Erik and Gunnar dismantled the left front-wheel assembly to discover that a locking pin in the drive-joint had dropped out due to it hitting

One of the classic pictures from the East African Safari, capturing Torsten Åman leading Erik Carlsson through one of the flooded sections on the 1966 event.

the stabilizer each time the wheel turned. Fortunately, among the spares carried they found a nut and bolt that fitted and the duo were soon on their way again, although by this time several competitors had overtaken them. All was not perfect, though, for the lower wishbone was held in place by only one bolt — there should have been two.

About 125 miles later they reached the service halt only to discover that the crew hadn't got the required spares. Undaunted, Erik and Gunnar set off again safe in the knowledge that the service crew would have the parts when they passed that spot on their way north. By the time they reached Dar-es-Salaam several journalists had picked up the story, and as Erik and Gunnar explained what had happened the locals suddenly realized the Swedes had hit an ant-eater or 'muhanga'. Back home in Sweden, Erik's run-in with the 'muhanga'

No wonder Erik looks rather worried. His car was badly scarred by the time he reached the control at Dar-es-Salaam on the 1962 East African Safari. Below, an aerial view of a Saab on Safari, only in those days aircraft were strictly for photographers, not service crews.

There are many roads in East Africa, and many ways of getting lost on the Safari. Below, rally car service in the traditional way, with mechanics working without the support of light aircraft.

made the front page of the newspapers.

Erik and Gunnar's rally ended just outside Dar-es-Salaam when their half-hearted repair gave up for good and the left front wheel fell off.

Once again the Swedish press picked up the story and accused Erik of using the 'muhanga' as an excuse. Nevertheless, SAAB got plenty of good press coverage from the Safari, as was to happen again in 1964.

The 1964 Safari was one of the worst ever, with torrential rain making life very difficult for the competitors. On reaching Mbulu they found the road had been destroyed by lorries, so Erik left the road to drive along the banking. It was a trick that had worked successfully during their recce, but this time they got stuck. Gunnar then had the bright idea of rolling the Saab down the bank. So, with the aid of some locals, accompanied by loud protestations from Erik, they proceeded to do just that and managed to get the car back on all four wheels with only one broken headlight and a cracked windscreen as evidence.

They had barely crossed the Tanzanian border when they were stuck for three hours because of the rain. Visibility was zero and the water rose

In 1965 Erik Carlsson took along his brother-in-law Stirling Moss to co-drive for him on the Safari, but they lost their chances early on when their trip meter failed.

half-way up the doors; the only dry place in the Saab was behind the sun-visors, where Gunnar kept his maps. Finally, the rains subsided and Erik and Gunnar started pushing the car through the water, often with the water coming up to their chests. When they finally got moving they drove with the car's doors open in an effort to dry-out the interior. Between Dar-es-Salaam and Nairobi they stopped 40 times to dry out the distributor, and towards the end they were cadging dry cloth off the locals to dry the engine out.

Erik, Gunnar and Saab followed a Ford home, victory this time having been denied them by the rains. But it didn't matter, everyone had heard about the Swedes rolling the car out of trouble; could they prove it for the press photographers? They did, in front of Nairobi's town hall.

The winning Ford team found this a bit hard to swallow and so they tried to emulate SAAB's feat. Unfortunately, it didn't succeed for as they turned the winning Ford over on the town hall's dance floor there was the ominous tinkling of breaking glass accompanied by a steady stream of oil and battery acid out of the car. No one, particularly Ford, was very amused by the stunt. For the 1965

Berndt 'Malin' Melin — one of SAAB's super mechanics — had the chance of his life when he took over Tom Trana's car in the 1971 Safari after Tom had fallen ill. Despite a one-hour 'off' he managed to finish in 18th place.

Safari, Erik invited his brother-in-law — one Stirling Moss — to co-drive for him. What a combination, the uncrowned kings of rallying and racing! Stirling cut all the maps up and put them together on a roll of paper in a similar manner to the way Denis Jenkinson wrote his notes for their classic 1955 Mille Miglia drive. It worked well enough until the Halda Tripmaster packed up, but with a broken Trip and only strips of maps to help them the leading pair were hopelessly lost and out of the rally. As a sequel to that episode, Competitions Manager Bosse Hellberg received a telephone call in the middle of nowhere from a Swedish journalist wanting the story for his newspaper — the journalist was phoning from Sweden as well!

Erik's last attempt on the Safari was in 1966, when he had his comfortable lead snatched away from him when a stone holed the block. After that SAAB quit the Safari until 1971, when they returned with Tom Trana and Stig Blomqvist as drivers. Trana never made the start of the rally, though, as he fell ill two days before the event started, and it was then that SAAB mechanic Berndt 'Malin' Melin got his chance.

Malin is part of the inventory at the SAAB Competitions Department. His first rally with SAAB was in 1952 at the age of 14 when he was a 'mechanic' on a championship event in Southern Sweden. Mechanic is rather a grandiose title, for Malin's task was to wait with a can of petrol for Erik; his wait lasted 22 hours before Erik collected him and took him back to Trollhättan. But he didn't complain, and later he joined SAAB full-time and has been there ever since.

Malin had proved his driving ability in 1969 and 1970 when he had joined Erik and his co-driver Torsten Åman on the Baja 1000. SAAB now offered him his big chance, Tom's car in the Safari.

A quick telegram to the Swedish Federation soon secured him a licence and Malin was allowed to start the Safari.

If it had been a Hollywood script Malin would have won, but he didn't. He had an 'off', which cost him a hour, but he still managed 18th place out of 33 finishers, beating the great Timo Mäkinen on the way — a fact he doesn't let Mäkinen forget! Stig Blomqvist eventually finished 13th after changing the gearbox twice and losing a front wheel.

In six starts with 10 cars SAAB scored a second, a third, a sixth, a 13th and an 18th in the East African Safari Rally. Not such a bad record after all, especially if you count all the newspaper coverage.

Stig Blomqvist took 13th place on the 1971 Safari despite having to change his gearbox twice during the event.

Chapter 10

The professionals in Monte Carlo

If you asked a man in the street to name a rally for you he would most probably reply, 'Monte Carlo'. Although its importance within rallying has waxed and waned over the years it is still one of the public's favourites. It deserves to be, since it is the oldest of its kind in the world.

The 'Monte' was first run in 1911 as a publicity stunt organized by the little principality to drum up winter business for the hotels. In the early years of the century, motorists were considered as rather eccentric and the type of people who would like a holiday in the middle of winter — especially if they could drive there. Twenty-three cars were entered into that first event, victory eventually going to Henri Rougier in his Turcat Mery. The following year the entry was up to 87 cars, and so it went on, with a break during the war years, until 1924, when the Monte resumed as the most popular international rally.

Admittedly there were other events, but the Monte was the only true international, and it remained basically unchanged until the fifties. It must be remembered that until 1959 the RAC Rally was a navigational event, without any special stages, and the Swedish Rally, although designated an International, was strictly for local drivers.

On December 12, 1949, the first Saab rolled off the Trollhättan assembly line and little more than a month later Rolf Mellde and Greta Molander drove two Saabs in the Monte Carlo Rally. Greta finished 55th and Rolf 69th overall, although neither was allowed to do the final loop. Mellde attempted the Monte a couple of times after that, but SAAB's success was moderate — the cars just weren't competitive enough.

Erik Carlsson's first attempt on the Monte was made in 1960 with John Sprinzel as navigator. This was the last year of secret controls and Erik was early into most of them, simply because he drove too fast. The only control they were late at was in Monte Carlo itself, where they lost a minute in the town! Nevertheless they finished ninth overall.

It proved a valuable lesson to Erik as he discovered that you really needed a four-speed gearbox for the event. The following year, 1961, he used a Saab 95 estate car which was the only Saab produced with a four-speed 'box. Like all the rally cars it was prepared in Trollhättan before being shipped to Stockholm in plenty of time for the start. Then in stepped the Marketing Department, who told Competitions that the 1961 Saab 95 would have a slot at the back to keep the rear window clear — Erik's car must have that slot. So the mechanics set about modifying the car, cutting holes, grading the metal and repainting it, even replacing all the cables as the original ones melted when the paint was cured.

Two days before the start they got another message from the Marketing Department. 'The new car won't be ready, you've got to change the car back to its original form. . . .'

'When we started to drive, I couldn't tell the difference between the estate car and the normal 96,' Erik recalls, 'they felt identical. We pulled ahead from the French Panhard team like hell and that year the rules were made to suit the small car. But when the French organizers realized what would happen they simply added a 10 per cent handicap on all cars with two-stroke engines! That meant we finished fourth behind the Panhards. . . . 'Furthermore, we used Dunlop tyres with studs bolted from the inside and then there was no snow. We punctured tyre after tyre as the studs got hot by the friction on the dry roads.

A typically snowy setting for SAAB's debut in the Monte Carlo Rally.

When we reached the finish we had only one tyre with air in it.'

Then came 1962, and outright victory for Erik, partnered this time by Gunnar 'Twinkle' Häggbom. (Gunnar's nickname was coined by Pat Moss-Carlsson after the nursery rhyme, 'Twinkle, twinkle little star'.) It was an event which Erik remembers with affection. 'We enjoyed it tremendously and it was a real surprise for everyone. But then again, the 1962 event was a very difficult one and that suited the Saab.

'The real problems started after the event. People are very proper down in Monaco and you have to wear a dinner jacket at the prizegiving. I had taken mine but Gunnar hadn't — he thought a dark suit would do, but it didn't. We had to rent a dinner suit from one of the waiters at the Casino before they would let him in.' It was during that year that SAAB started the world's first professional rally team.

'Do you want to join me for the German rally?' Erik asked when he met Gunnar Palm at a race outside Stockholm. There could only be one answer. The pair finished second on the Baden-Baden rally behind the Porsche of Hans-Joachim Walter, and Erik was pleased enough with Gunnar's performance to offer him a seat on the 1963 Monte Carlo.

In the meantime, Gunnar Häggbom, who spoke fluent French, got a contract with Ford. It was the year Ford planned to conquer Europe with their Falcon Sprints, Graham Hill and Bo Ljungfeldt doing the driving. Gunnar Palm took leave from his job as a washing-machine salesman and started to prepare for the event like no-one had done before.

'I knew that Erik was most ambitious and I had decided that he shouldn't be dissatisfied.' Palm worked with maps, the *Guide Michelin* and his notes from the previous year, when he had done the Monte with Bjarne Lundberg in his Jaguar.

At the same time SAAB's Competition Department was being formed in Trollhättan under the supervision of Bo Hellberg, who joined the Company in March, 1962. Hellberg planned the service, with Pelle Rudh and Sven Olsson acting as mechanics. Hellberg would be there as well — they were out for a second victory. And win they did, although it was by no means easy.

They hadn't practised the road sections down to Chambéry and it proved difficult to find the shortest route as there had been heavy falls of snow. Cars were getting stuck everywhere, including the Ford Falcon Futura Sprint of Bo Ljungfeldt/Gunnar Häggbom, who were heavily penalized and had virtually lost the rally even before it had started. Somehow the Saab struggled through it all,

Rolf Mellde and Greta Molander, who were regular competitors on the Monte Carlo Rally in the early-fifties, pose for a celebratory picture having reached the Principality with their cars intact.

although not without road penalties. After Chambéry came the freezing rain, with the competitors leaving the road left, right and centre; it was so slippery that people couldn't walk on the road once their car had gone off. Erik had his own problems with the Saab's carburettors freezing up.

On top of everything else the car was consuming enormous amounts of petrol because of the icing, and they eventually ran out of fuel. It was veteran driver Olle Dahl who came to their rescue by pushing them into the time control at Bedouin before Mont Ventoux. 'We would probably still have been there,' Gunnar said. 'Olle damaged his extra lights to help us get in at the last minute. We

Erik Carlsson used the Saab 95 estate car for the 1961 Monte Carlo Rally as at that time it was the only model with a four-speed gearbox.

Erik's first outright victory in the Monte came in 1962, when he was partnered by Gunnar Häggbom.

53

The winning car in action on the 1962 Monte, tackling the round-the-houses test and one of the snow-covered sections high above Monaco.

managed it, but in my haste I nearly tipped up the whole of the time control — tables, the lot.'

'I like that Mr. Palm,' was Erik's only remark when he saw Gunnar's unintentional attack on the officials!

As the car was consuming twice as much petrol as it should, Erik and Gunnar realised they needed some alcohol to keep the carburettors from freezing-up but they couldn't find any. So Erik took it very steadily down to Monte Carlo going for a good placing rather than victory.

The Mont Ventoux stage was extremely slippery and Erik wasn't at all happy about his driving, nevertheless they made it to the summit and down to the coast, where they knocked an inch of solid ice off the car. Despite Erik's reservations about his driving he had done enough to win.

Many of their fellow competitors had withdrawn when they got stuck in the snow and ditches unable to see where they were going. The cars' defrosters simply couldn't cope with the ice. 'It was an incredible feeling to win like that,' recalls Gunnar. 'It wasn't only the sun that made us blink at the prize ceremony.' The only problem was that the organizers played 'The King's Song' instead of the Swedish National Antham, a tradition they haven't changed, although when Björn Waldegård won in 1969 they started off with the Swiss National Anthem before changing to 'The King's Song'.

On their return to Sweden, the victorious duo were fêted at a reception held by SAAB's Managing Director, Tryggve Holm. It was then that Gunnar was asked to do the Finnish Hankki rally with Erik, but he refused because of his job, and it was only after this that Gunnar became an employee of SAAB, working for the Public Relations Depart-

ment in Nyköping, and co-driving for Erik Carlsson on rallies. His salary wasn't very big, but he did get a 2,000 Crowns bonus (then about £200) per event. As an aside Erik had joined SAAB on March 15, 1956, as a test driver and became an employee of the Competitions Department when SAAB took over the Swedish dealer organization ANA (AB Nyköpings Automobilfabrik) in 1960.

Back to the Monte. In 1964, Erik came third after a rally-long battle with the Finns and Minis, although it was Irishman Paddy Hopkirk who eventually won, while the following year Erik could do no better than 16th; this event also marked the end of his partnership with Gunnar Palm. They were in the lead when they came into Chambéry and a quarrel started. By now the Saab had extra air intakes on the bonnet to keep the engine cool. On the run down to Chambéry these intakes had been covered up, but now Erik wanted to remove them. Gunnar wasn't so sure, bearing in mind that the Competitions Department's foreman, Paul Broman, had advised them not to remove the covers if there was a chance of snow. But Erik would have none of it and so off came the covers.

Inevitably it snowed on the Col du Granier stage, and the Saab barely reached the start. Immediately after the start they had to stop and change spark plugs and Gunnar had to push the car uphill. After a long stop in order to get the snow out of the engine compartment they finally reached the finish having lost 58 minutes in 26 miles, and the fight between Erik and Gunnar really got going.

One Mini after another passed the fraught Swedish pair and the organizers in Monte Carlo simply

Erik returned to Monte Carlo in 1963 for a second victory, this time carrying another competition number, 283, and another co-driver, Gunnar Palm.

couldn't believe Erik's time for the first stage, so they promptly lopped an hour off it and made Erik the leader. It was soon changed back, though.

On the final 372-miles loop in the mountains to the north of Monte Carlo Erik was the only driver not to be penalized on the road, but it wasn't enough. They finished 16th and the Carlsson/Palm partnership was at an end. From there on Torsten Åman became Erik's regular co-driver, while Gunnar went with Åke Andersson in one of the other factory Saabs.

The 1965 Monte marked the end of SAAB's official involvement with that particular rally, although many privateers continued to compete in the event with two-strokes and, later on, V4s. One of them was Sture Nottorp, the man behind SAAB's entry in the 1959 Le Mans. Ten years after that he entered Simo Lampinen in a Sonett II, encouraged by Tom Trana's 10th place the preceding year in a 96.

Lampinen was in good form, having won the RAC for SAAB in 1968, and after three special stages on the Monte he was third in class behind two Porsches, one of which was driven by Björn Waldegård. But Simo was to become a victim of the organizers' habit of breaking the rules to suit the French. Simo passed a time control without doing any service, as others did, the SAAB service point being located just before the next time control. The organizers hadn't calculated their time schedule to cope with this, and when Simo swept along the road as the first car one of the passage controls wasn't put up. Everything was there, marshals, the table, stamp, etc, but no sign at the roadside. Nevertheless, the marshals noted Simo's starting number as he passed.

On arriving at Monte Carlo he and Bo Hellberg took the matter up with the chairman of the organizing committee, who assured them that everything would be all right. But when the results were published Simo's name was excluded. When everyone asked why, the organizers claimed he had missed a passage control! The real reason was that Simo was too close behind the French favourite, Gerard Larrousse in his Porsche. Understandably, Sture Nottorp was rather upset by this decision, and had to be physically restrained by Bo Hellberg.

Saabs in the snow on the way to Monaco. Top, the Norwegian driver Arne Ingier on the 1963 event. Centre, prolific ladies' award winner Pat Moss-Carlsson in 1964. Right, Ove Andersson and Torsten Åman, who could have finished high-up in 1965 until a broken gear lever dropped them to 12th place.

The super-smooth Finnish driver Simo Lampinen entered the 1969 Monte in a semi-private capacity with a Sonett II and was doing so well with it that he passed a passage control before it was fully operational, the organizers having miscalculated their own time schedule. Though assured that all would be well, he was subsequently excluded from the official results.

Chapter 11

Formula cars without success

There were no boundaries for the technicians at SAAB in the early days, and experiments and developments were carried out in every corner of the factory. Some worked, others didn't, and one that didn't is affectionately known as the 'Monster'. The Monster was basically a 93 body-shell with the engine compartment slightly widened to house twin three-cylinder units coupled to a joint transmission.

'It was as quick as hell in a straight line,' recalls Erik Carlsson, 'but a bastard to steer, and so the project was dropped.' The Monster is now residing in the SAAB museum at Trollhättan.

One experiment that gained more publicity was the Saab Formula Junior racing car. Formula Junior was a small, relatively cheap, class for monoposto racers with an engine capacity of no more than 1,000 cc. It was recognized by the FIA in 1959 and was to substitute the old 500 cc Formula 3. It was a success right from the start, though there were few of the privately built cars that the Formula's initiators, Juan-Manuel Fangio and Count Giovanni Lurani, had hoped for, and the class soon became the property of established teams from Lotus, Lola, Elva and Stanguellini.

SAAB entered the scene with a unique design. Unlike their competitors, the Saab Junior had an aluminium monocoque, while in front of the front wheels there was a three-cylinder two-stroke engine mounted on its side with the gearbox behind it. Power output from the 940 cc engine, fed by twin Solex carburettors, was 90 bhp at 7,000 rpm. Bodywork was made from glass-fibre.

As the engineers were only permitted to go ahead with the project if they used as many standard parts as possible, the suspension and chassis components came from road-going Saabs, with the springs inverted to make the car as low as possible. And it went. Top speed was close to 130 mph — in a straight line. But, like the Monster, it suffered from terminal understeer at corners — after all, 70 per cent of the car's weight was over the front wheels. 'You had to start to turn some 30 to 40 metres before a bend and still you couldn't be sure of making it when you were there,' Erik Carlsson recalls. The results weren't as bad as one might suspect, though.

It made its debut in May 1961 at the Finnish Djurgårdsloppet, outside Helsingfors. Carl-Magnus Skogh was fourth and Erik Carlsson fifth, with the Finnish ace, Carl-Otto Bremer winning. At Denmark's Roskilde Ring later in the year Carl-Magnus held second place until electrical troubles stopped him, and at the Gelleråsen circuit, near Karlskoga, Erik's car suffered from fuel problems, while Carl-Magnus was pushed off by Ynge Rosqvist in a Cooper just as Carl-Magnus was about to overtake him. When the annual race in Flakenberg, 'The West Coastal Race', was held in July, SAAB found themselves with a real fight on their hands when Finland's Curt Lincoln turned up with a brand new Cooper. Erik takes over the story:

'We really had a fight. He pulled ahead right from the start, but with all my weight over the front wheels I had no difficulty outbraking him into turns. Then he would get away again and I would outbrake him, but in the end it was too much and he got too far in front of me.

'Furthermore, it was that understeer. No, I don't think that a real racing car should have front-wheel drive.'

This is not the end of the story, though, for in the 1960s some American enthusiasts produced the

Above, Gösta Karlsson demonstrates the extreme understeer of the original Saab Junior single-seater, and evidence of nose damage to which the unsatisfactory handling probably contributed. With so much weight ahead of the front wheels, below, the understeer was inevitable. Right and right below, a later application of the three-cylinder Saab engine to single-seater racing.

A Saab engine was used to power this attractive British Formula 4 racer, but the project was not developed.

Quantam. This, too, was a Formula car, similar to Formula Vee, with the engine behind the driver. SAAB Sweden showed some interest in the project, and one car reached Sweden before funds ran out and the project was stopped. Some years later, the spectators at Karlskoga saw a demonstration of a British Formula 4 racer fitted with a SAAB engine, but that died too.

Today, the Saab Formula Junior car rests in SAAB's museum, still in perfect racing condition, as a reminder of a brave but abortive effort to produce a competitive front-drive monoposto.

Chapter 12

Ten victories out of 29 starts

The Saab made its debut as a rally car in 1950, the year the Swedish Rally was inaugurated. SAAB and Rolf Mellde's prime ambition then was to win the Swedish Rally to the Midnight Sun, as it was then called.

In those days the rally was run in the middle of the summer to Kiruna in the far north — the land of the midnight sun. In the end it took SAAB 10 years of trying before they finally scored that victory. Mellde entered the event 11 times, and finished 11 times, but he never made it to the winner's rostrum. The first SAAB victory in this event went to Erik Carlsson (who else?) in 1959.

On his first attempt Mellde was second in class behind the German Prince von Fürstenberg. Two years later Mellde, Molander and Blomberg took the first three places in their class, and in 1955 Greta Molander took the ladies' class for the fourth time. Class wins were easy, but outright victory proved a little more difficult as during the fifties the rules favoured the larger cars such as the Porsches.

All that changed in 1956, when the big cars became a disadvantage and it was the turn of VW to have the upper hand. Carl-Magnus Skogh managed third overall that year and Saabs filled the top 25 places in their class!

SAAB's first victory should have come in 1958, but the three young drivers, Carl-Magnus Skogh, Erik Carlsson and Carl Orrenius, all went off on the same bend (that must be some kind of record in itself). Carl-Magnus was the first to go off, and the spectators wanted to warn the other drivers, but Carl-Magnus stopped them on the grounds that all the drivers should have the same disadvantage. Carlsson was the second to go off and Orrenius the third. Carl-Magnus eventually got his car

restarted, but the other two were out of the rally. Although Mellde and Molander took a one-two in the class, overall victory still eluded SAAB.

The breakthrough came in 1959 with Erik gaining a perfect, trouble-free victory. 'I have never seen the SAAB management as happy after any other victory,' Erik says, which wasn't surprising as there were at least 25 drivers capable of winning the event.

Erik's victory opened the door for SAAB as Carl-Magnus Skogh won in 1960 and 1961, when Erik was trying too hard. In 1961 Erik (co-driven by Mario Pavoni) jumped the start on a stage and was penalized 60 seconds, but by the last stage he had virtually made it up — he was only two seconds behind the Porsche of Berndt Jansson. Mellde encouraged Erik to catch Jansson, rather than be content with what he had already achieved, which was all Erik needed. On one of the notorious 'yumps' on the classic Husås-Andviken stage his car took off, rolled on landing and slammed into a telegraph pole at some 87 mph. Apart from injured pride he and his co-driver were all right, while the only thing salvagable from the car was the Halda Speedpilot which they returned to Mellde who was still at the start of the stage, which then had to be cancelled as the accident had brought down the telephone cable linking the start and finish.

Erik left the road again in 1961, on this occasion to avoid a collision with another car, but by this time new drivers, such as Åke 'The Brewer' Andersson, were beginning to make their presence felt (Åke's father owned a brewery). Åke was extremely rapid, but more often than not he prematurely finished rallies with his Saab inverted. He started the 1964 Midnight Sun rally like a madman, the first stages being run on his home

Erik Carlsson on the classic Husås-Andviken stage of the Swedish Rally to the Midnight Sun during the 1956 event.

Rolf Mellde raises the dust on one of his first attempts to win Sweden's major rally.

ground around Uppsala, to the north of Stockholm. Erik wasn't impressed by this and when the rally reached the Tierp airfield he thought he would show young Andersson a thing or two, and he certainly did; 10 metres before the finish line he rolled the car in front of thousands of spectators, eventually stopping on the left door. Gunnar Palm clambered out through the other door and, with Erik's help from within the car, managed to get it back on to four wheels, having lost a minute; Gunnar finished the stage sitting on the car's bonnet!

Erik needn't have worried, though, for Ake didn't win the rally, which went to Tom Trana, driving a Volvo. The best-placed Saab driver was

62

Ove Andersson, who came fourth.

Åke was second to Trana in 1965, before getting a well-deserved victory in 1966. In 1965 the organizers changed the timing of the rally from summer to winter and the year that Åke won proved to be one of the coldest ever. The temperature dropped to −43 degrees Celsius and the mechanics had their time cut out just keeping the cars going. While Åke was leading, Erik's co-driver, Torsten Åman, found a short-cut through some woods — a route used only by the SAAB team — but unfortunately the engine of their car seized and they were stranded. 'We were just about to strip the car's interior to light a fire', Erik remembers, 'when Simo Lampinen came along and gave us a lift to the nearest village.' There Erik and Torsten met another competitor and talked him into retiring so that he could give the SAAB duo a lift back to civilization! Åke Andersson won this event with Simo Lampinen second, Carl Orrenius fourth and Pat Moss taking the ladies' prize, so with or without Erik Carlsson the Saabs did well in Sweden.

Rolf Mellde poses with one of his earliest rally cars, and below, Erik Carlsson driving to victory in the 1959 Swedish Rally with a Group 3 Saab 93.

63

Carl-Magnus Skogh, who was victorious on the Swedish event in 1960 and 1961.

Then along came Björn Waldegård with his Porsche, and SAAB had to be content with a couple of seconds scored by Simo Lampinen. Other Saab drivers who took second places behind Waldegård include Tom Trana — who left Volvo for SAAB in 1967 — and Håkan Lindberg, who had been one of Sweden's top navigators before starting to drive in 1964. In 1970 he rolled his Saab twice during the Swedish Rally but still managed to come second.

Behind drivers like these, Stig Blomqvist started to make a name for himself on the Swedish Rally, his impressive score being 1968, 9th; 1969, 8th;

1970, 3rd; 1971, victory. Including the 1980 event Stig has only since been beaten three times in the Swedish Rally. In 1974 the event was cancelled due to the oil crisis, in 1975 Waldegård won in the ultimate rally car — the Lancia Stratos — and in 1976 Stig's arch-rival, Per Eklund, won after one of the most thrilling rallies ever.

The event was only a couple of stages old when it became apparent to the spectators that Stig and Per were going hell for leather — no-one else was ever going to get a look-in. At the halfway stop Per led Stig by just 14 seconds! 'The worst situation I've ever been in,' Bo Hellberg says, 'I couldn't tell the

Monte Carlo, a colourful
background for the final round-
the-houses test of the famous
rally, which Eric Carlsson first
entered in 1960 and won
outright two years later.

The Saab Junior, an interesting
but not particularly successful
foray by the Swedish company
into single-seater racing.

A couple of problems for Stig Blomqvist. With front-wheel drive the loss of a rear wheel on a special stage did not delay him unduly, but when his 96 V4 had an argument with a park bench in Sutton Park on the 1972 RAC Rally he had to reverse his way out of trouble.

Erik Carlsson tried just a bit too hard
on the Tierp airfield in 1964 . . .

boys to hold back — they were both driving to the best of their ability, and the cars, now producing some 145 bhp, were running better than ever.'

The fact that Stig's car had a puncture didn't help matters, either, as it put him well behind Per. On one stage towards the end of the rally he started the stage before Per, but about three miles in he had a slight 'off' and before he regained the road he could see Per's lights bearing down on him. Stig immediately doused his lights, except for his spots, so that Per wouldn't be given any help, and then drove on. 'At least I didn't give him any extra

help,' Stig smiled afterwards.

Per was a very popular winner, some people even suggesting that he should become Sir Per of Värmland, but things like that don't happen in Sweden. Immediately after the rally, Per's car was taken to the SAAB museum, where it rests today.

Ten victories for SAAB in 29 years is a virtually unbeatable record. The win in 1979 was perhaps the most signficant as Stig Blomqvist and Björn Cederberg took the Group 4 99 Turbo two-door to its first victory — the first international win for a turbocharged rally car. Things like this are needed to give life to rallying, which is becoming more professional and, perhaps, a bit duller as a result. A lot has changed since Mellde's days of 25 bhp two-strokes, but even in the modern world of ultra-professionalism and technical sophistication rallying is still essentially a genuine sport.

Top left, Olle Bromark lifts a wheel. Top, Pat Moss takes a tight line. Above, Håkan Lindberg was always quick, even when he had lost part of a tyre. Below, The Swedish Rally changed from a summer to a winter event in 1965. This is Åke Andersson on the 1967 event.

Above, Arne Hertz and Stig Blomqvist celebrate victory in the 1971 Swedish Rally in Gothenburg. Below and right, Per Eklund fought off Stig's every trick to win the 1976 event, when practice was banned and Saabs were invincible. Centre right, Stig took the 16-valve 99 to victory in 1977 and, bottom, his 1979 success was his fifth and his first with a Turbo.

Chapter 13

Carl-Magnus Skogh — a true finisher

While Erik was establishing his reputation as one of Sweden's most spectacular rally drivers, who very often finished rallies earlier than intended, Carl-Magnus Skogh was building his rallying career in exactly the opposite way — he was one of the smoothest rally drivers seen, rarely damaging his car or retiring from events. While Erik was travelling Europe, dominating the RAC and Monte Carlo rallies, Carl-Magnus dominated the Scandinavian rallying scene in a way that has yet to be emulated.

Carl-Magnus was 25 before he made his rallying debut; prior to that he had tried cross-country running, ski-ing and athletics. He had even played football in the third division for Dalsland. By profession he was a forester, so he had to do a lot of driving on back roads, and it was while he was doing this that he realised it was what he enjoyed the most. His first event was the Dalslandsloppet in 1954, in which he came third. After that he entered championship rallies, and in his first year he finished 16th overall and gained a fifth on the lengendary Rikspokalen.

In 1957 he won the Rikspokalen outright; without the aid of any studs or chains he averaged 35 mph over the very slippery stages. By 1961 Carl-Magnus had won the Rikspokalen three times to become the only driver to keep the silver trophy for good.

He was a most reliable driver, whose motto of 'safety first' ensured that he finished the Swedish Rally no lower than fourth on all the times he entered it, winning that event two years on the trot in 1960 and 1961 after finishing second to Erik in 1959. It was a one-two that shook the Swedish Volkswagen team.

Living close to the Norwegian border, Carl-Magnus crossed it frequently to compete in their events, and his favourite was the Viking Rally, which he won three times; he also rolled his car on that event. The Viking Rally was a round of the Scandinavian Championship, which Carl-Magnus won outright twice and was fourth twice.

In Sweden he was a very difficult man to beat, and when he did venture abroad his results were quite respectable, winning the Polish Rally outright and coming third in the Tulip Rally. But for some reason he never got the same headlines as Erik Carlsson.

Carl-Magnus Skogh, who did so much to enhance SAAB's competition record.

Carl-Magnus was invited to demonstrate the new Sonett to the press in 1956, and in 1960 he was employed by SAAB as a test driver. Like most drivers in those days he went racing on Sundays when there was no rallies, and he did quite well, beating Erik Carlsson and Rolf Mellde in the new four-speed Group 3 93s in his first race at the Karlskoga track, despite being handicapped by having an older three-speed car.

He also gave the Saab Formula Junior its first ever victory, at the Skarpnäck airfield on the outskirts of Stockholm. Skarpnäck was a classic circuit that had been used for Grand Prix racing since 1948. Mellde and Skogh also drove a Saab to victory in Sweden's first 12-hours race for production saloons, which was held at the same circuit.

He was well known and appreciated, and everyone in West Sweden knew his car's registration number, P9293. But he never gained the fame he deserved. By the end of 1962 SAAB had two star drivers, Erik Carlsson and Carl-Magnus Skogh, but that was one too many, and Carl-Magnus moved to Volvo, where he rallied the 544 and 122 with varying success.

Swedish rally roads are often very similar to British forestry stages. Here is Skogh on his way to victory in the 1960 Rikspokalen.

Carl-Magnus was partnered by his brother Rolf for many years.

The Skogh brothers were success- ful in winning one international rally outright – the Polish.

Carl-Magnus drove the Formula Junior Saab in a couple of races, but gave it up after having been pushed off at Karlskoga in 1960.

Chapter 14

The RAC Rally — one of the best

The British contribution to international rallying, the RAC Rally, has always been a firm favourite with the SAAB team. Until 1959, the RAC was virtually unheard-of, as in those days it was a four-day navigational exercise. Furthermore, it was run in November and at that time of the year, there are warmer places to be than in the British Isles! However, that year saw things change. Jack Kemsley, one of the leading lights of the organizing committee, decided that the Continental way of running rallies, that is over special stages, would enhance the RAC Rally and attract overseas competitors. Today, the RAC Rally is one of the world's top three events and one to which SAAB always go.

Nobody can recall who suggested to Rolf Mellde that Saabs would be well suited to the RAC, but whoever it was, SAAB owe them a great deal. Without Erik Carlsson's three straight victories in 1960, 1961 and 1962 it would have been very difficult for the young Swedish company to get a foothold in the UK market, for in those days the distinctive smell of the two-stroke petroil mixture wasn't appreciated by the British motorist. Twenty years later, the UK is SAAB's second most important export market after the United States.

SAAB first entered the RAC in 1959, when Erik Carlsson was partnered by John Sprinzel, but despite his experience, co-driving for Erik was completely alien to the way John was used to doing things. Gone was the open-top sports car and being buffeted by the elements, and here was a giant of a man who wound the windows up, put the heater on full and drove every stage as though it were to be his last. But it nearly worked first time out.

It was perfect Saab weather, with plenty of snow everywhere and very slippery stages. Not surpris-

ingly, Erik was fastest on every stage, but then disaster struck with only 60 miles to go. In avoiding a collision with a private car, Erik swerved and drove the Saab straight into an unremitting bridge — it was the end of his rally.

It also spelt the end of Erik's attempt on the European Championship (a title he never held), as he was disqualified a few weeks later for having the door numbers in the wrong colour. . . . The following year, 1960, Erik made no mistakes and partnered by Stuart Turner he won the event with ease, leading the way for a whole string of Scandinavian drivers who have virtually dominated the RAC ever since.

Stories abound of Erik's rallying adventures, but one is a classic from the 1962 RAC and illustrates the sort of problems a foreign entrant could get into (remember there weren't the number of service crews in those days that there are now).

On the very last stage, the Saab's rear trailing-arm broke and it would have proved impossible to reach the next time control. It looked as though Erik and co-driver David Stone were out of the rally, but then Erik spotted a brand new Saab parked by the stage — locked and with the owner out of sight. Without more ado Erik and David jacked the car up and removed the wanted trailing-arm and fixed it to their car, leaving an explanatory note under the now immobile car's windscreen wiper. Unfortunately, just as they were about to leave the scene of the crime, the car's owner turned up and it took all of Erik's not inconsiderable persuasive powers to get away with it. Eventually, the aggrieved owner let them go on their way to win the event and, subsequently, he and Erik have become firm friends.

Following Erik's victory in 1962, the little two-

Erik Carlsson and co-driver Stuart Turner parade in their victorious Saab after the 1960 RAC Rally before a well-dressed audience at a London hotel.

In 1961 slalom tests still played a decisive part in the RAC Rally.

strokes were losing their competitiveness and in the next three years the best Erik and SAAB could manage was third, seventh and fourth places.

For the 1966 RAC, the Trollhättan Competitions Department gave Erik the quickest two-stroke yet. From its 841 cc engine it produced 84.6 bhp, but that still wasn't enough and the old two-stroke was pensioned-off.

Saab sales generally were beginning to decline because of the growing unpopularity of the two-stroke engine. However, SAAB didn't possess the finance to build their own four-stroke engine to replace it, so after looking at Wankel engines, Lancia's narrow V4 and Ford of Germany's V4, the Swedes decided that the latter would be the best, and this engine was used in the Saab 96s from then on. For the 1967 RAC the engine was tuned to produce 105 bhp, but there was more to come as we shall see.

The RAC was cancelled that year due to a foot and mouth epidemic and the risk that the cars might spread it further round the country. However, the organizers invited the top drivers to drive

72

over one special stage for the TV, and Erik won to give the V4-powered Saab some much-needed publicity in the UK.

New drivers were now beginning to take over as the years caught up with Erik. The 1968 RAC was won by the Finnish driver Simo Lampinen, who took his 122 bhp V4 into the lead after only four of the 60 stages; not even team-mate Carl Orrenius could keep up with him. Simo's 1968 RAC victory was to launch him on a long and illustrious rallying career that was to last for a further 11 years until 1979, when he retired after that year's RAC.

Simo had suffered from polio as a boy and this had left him with a weak leg which made it difficult for him to use the clutch on long rallies. He there-

When Erik was partnered by David Stone for the 1962 event, Lombank was already in the picture as sponsor of the RAC Rally.

Co-driver John Davenport and Simo Lampinen show off the magnificent RAC trophy which they were awarded for victory in 1968.

Lampinen cornering hard on a loose surface during the night with his victorious 125 bhp V4 during the 1968 event.

Celebrating SAAB's greatest RAC Rally success after the 1971 event. From left to right, Carl Orrenius (3rd), Stig Blomqvist (1st) and Per Eklund (7th) with their co-drivers behind them.

On his way to victory in 1971 Stig managed to perform this unscheduled stunt on a special stage.

fore made great use of the Saab's freewheel device, which meant he could change up or down without using the clutch.

Apart from Lampinen, Carl Orrenius was the only other SAAB driver to reach the finish, as both Håkan Lindberg and Tom Trana, who had joined SAAB a year earlier, retired with broken differentials. However, Orrenius' drive was anything but troublefree; on the first stage the carburettor started causing problems, while on the third stage the car landed very heavily after a 'yump' and Orrenius and his co-driver, Gustaf Schröderheim,

spent an anxious few minutes waiting for something to break. Fortunately nothing did, and they eventually finished second, the third-placed driver being more than an hour behind them. Orrenius repeated his second place in 1969, this time behind Harry Källström in the Lancia Fulvia.

1970 was a year SAAB would rather forget, however, as all four factory entries failed to finish and the best-placed SAAB driver was privateer Lasse Jönsson, who finished ninth. 'It is difficult to explain,' Bo Hellberg says, 'one year you are right on top and the next nothing works and yet your preparation is identical.' It was during that year that Stig Blomqvist, then aged 24, showed his true potential, leading the event until he hit a wall on the Great Orme stage and had to retire with a broken drive-shaft.

In 1971, though, it all came right for Stig and SAAB. Conditions for that year's RAC were as bad as ever. 'I started slowly, but Yorkshire was more or less paralysed because of all the snow, and I

Stig has invariably done well on the RAC Rally; he finished second in 1972, 1974 and 1976.

Above, Håkan Lindberg came home in fifth place in 1969. Below, Arne Hertz holds the champagne as he and Stig celebrate their 1971 victory.

realized I had a chance,' Stig recalls. 'Timo Mäkinen was quicker, but we let him run and stayed behind.' Stig's co-driver, Arne Hertz, now started to come into his own and played with the time allowances that were given. He succeeded in making them run as late as possible in order to let the other drivers clean the roads for them. As the rally headed for Scotland, Harry 'Sputnik' Källström was in the lead on the road, but without any real chance of leading overall.

When the event headed south again, Blomqvist, Orrenius and Per Eklund were in complete command, but then Per had an 'off', bending the rear axle right in front of a group of Swedish journalists, who had been brought to the event by SAAB's PR staff.

The SAAB mechanics heard about the problem over the radio and at the next time control they launched themselves at the cars; in 25 minutes they changed two back axles (Stig had had a slight off as well), plus a complete front-end. This was in addition to all the routine tasks such as changing brake pads, shock absorbers and wheels, and refuelling and topping-up with water. Stig went on to win the event with Orrenius third and Eklund seventh. Per did the last two stages with only third and fourth gears; his co-driver, Sölve Andreasson, had to get out of the car and push every time Per wanted to reverse.

SAAB won the team prize and, in addition to that, 52-year-old veteran Olle Dahl drove his own

Stig gets his car airborne on a special stage during the 1972 event, his car already somewhat bent, but not as badly as it was to be two years later, as can be seen on the previous page.

Ola Strömberg gained quite a reputation for this highly spectacular roll on the Sutton Park stage during the 1977 RAC Rally.

car to 16th place overall. That RAC victory capped a spectacular year for the 25-year-old Blomqvist, and established him as the leading front-wheel-drive exponent. In 1971, Stig started in 16 rallies and scored 11 wins, including the Swedish, the Finnish and, of course, the RAC. From 1972 the RAC has been dominated by Fords, with Roger Clark taking that first win. His 230 bhp, 16-valve Ford Escort was simply too powerful for Stig's 145 bhp Saab 96, which came in second.

SAAB tried to fight back and they made their last attempt with the 96 model in 1975, by which time fuel-injection had increased the power to 165 bhp, but it was too much and both cars broke down. In 1976 SAAB used the larger 99 for the first time, and but for a couple of punctures on the last stage Stig would have had his second RAC victory. Instead, he had to make do with second, once again behind Roger Clark.

By now SAAB also had a 16-valve engine, based on the 2-litre 99 block, which produced 225 bhp; every horsepower was needed as the 99 was a large and heavy car. By the end of 1977 the engine was useless as the regulations were changed so that 400 units had to be produced — too many for a small manufacturer like SAAB.

The Swedes had a secret weapon, though, which they were quietly working on. The Turbo. For the 1978 RAC, Stig and Per drove brand-new turbocharged Saab 99 Combi Coupes in Group 2 trim, the engines producing 240 bhp. Unfortunately, drive-shaft problems forced both cars out of the event, but not before they had shown their potential. On some of the tarmac stages Stig managed to beat Markku Álen's Lancia Stratos, so things augured well for the Turbo.

Following a year's development and the homologation into Group 2 of the Saab 99 Turbo two-door, SAAB were optimistic about the 1979 RAC Rally. Stig was joined on this event by 32-years-old Ola Strömberg, who drove a 240 bhp Turbo, compared with Stig's 270 bhp version. Ola had done the RAC once before in 1977, but had retired following a spectacular roll in Sutton Park; this time he felt more confident and was partnered by Bo Reinicke, one of Stig's old co-drivers. Both drivers made a promising start with Stig being right up amongst the leaders after the tarmac stages — usually a weak point with Saabs. But their rally was soon to end, with Ola Strömberg retiring with water pump failure and Stig having two of his very rare 'offs'.

Chapter 15

From 25 to 250 horsepower

Saab rally cars have come a long way from the original 25 bhp to the current 250-plus bhp models. During the 30 years that SAAB have been rallying, the cars from Trollhättan have always been underpowered compared with their competitors. It is only with the recent introduction of the Turbo that things have started to change.

Back in 1950 the base was the Saab 92 — a two-cylinder, two-stroke producing 25 bhp at 3,800 rpm from its 764 cc; the compression ratio was 6.6:1 and torque was 40.5 lb ft. A mechanical fuel pump fed a simple Solex carburettor with 4 per cent oil-mixed petrol. The engine was water-cooled, but it lacked a water pump; the water was self-circulating, working on the 'thermosiphon' principle that hot water is lighter then cold.

The gearbox had three forward gears and featured a column-mounted gear-lever. A freewheel was standard in order to reduce fuel consumption and avoid seizing, as sometimes happens to two-strokes if used for braking in long downhill runs.

Brakes were hydraulic, but the brake area was not impressive at 91.9 sq in. The handbrake activated the rear drums mechanically, while the electrical system gave 6 volts with a 130-watt generator. These figures were not particularly impressive, but the pieces held together, and, above all, the Saab was aerodynamic with a low drag coefficient of just over 0.32. Like all Saabs to come the 92 had a very strong and heavy body.

It wasn't long before Rolf Mellde and his colleagues had tuned the new car. It was easy in those days as regulations were liberal and you were allowed to do more or less whatever you liked. Power soon reached 35 bhp, and in most rallies this was sufficient. The three-speed gearbox was not enough, though. The roads in those days were very twisty and the Saab drivers often had to shift down into first to get through a bend, whereas the rival Volkswagen drivers could use second. It was here that Saab drivers lost ground, but on fast winding roads they could make it up.

The handicap was eliminated by very late braking into bends. In fact the drivers got into the habit of not braking at all! And, most importantly, they never let up. Left-foot braking soon became a must for every Saab driver if he wanted to stay competitive. The principle was easy; just keep your right foot down and balance the car with your left foot on the brake pedal. Clutchless gear-changes were also the norm. This technique meant that you had to keep your left foot on the brake pedal all the time. But as the brake pedal was mounted quite high this was tiring and the drivers therefore put a big piece of wood on the floor on which to rest the left foot. Apart from a slightly tuned engine and a piece of wood, not much was done to the cars.

Later, the co-driver was given a new instrument — the Halda Speedpilot — which could be used to calculate average speeds on long rallies. This was essential as most rallies were run against the clock with frequent use of secret time controls.

In 1953 the Saab 92B was introduced. The standard engine now produced 28 bhp, a figure the rally cars had long passed. The car still featured torsion-bar suspension with slightly positive camber at the back. This gave the car somewhat peculiar behaviour when driven hard, but that was easily cured.

'I noticed it the first time during the Rally to the Midnight Sun, in 1950,' Rolf Mellde remembers. 'The car was suddenly very easy to drive in right-hand bends and when we checked it we noticed that the left side trailing-arm was broken. I then realized that we should have set the suspension for negative camber at the rear, and this was done in a special rig at the technical department.'

Other drivers used different methods. Erik Carlsson quite simply invited a couple of friends to come along for a ride, he then took the car over some of the worse 'yumps' he could find. His back-seat passengers liked the performance and the suspension was adequately modified! The engine output was slowly raised, and when the two-cylinder was replaced at the end of 1955 it produced close to 50 bhp, but as Erik Carlsson recalls, 'that was in pure racing form'.

Then along came the 93, with a three-cylinder engine placed longitudinally in the car. Although the capacity was smaller, at only 748 cc, the output was greater at 33 bhp in standard form. The gear-box was new, but still only three-speed, while the cooling system was now fitted with the long awaited water pump, and the chassis featured coil springs all round instead of the torsion-bars. This, combined with a slightly wider track, worked miracles for the car's handling, and the new engine's greater torque made the 93 a delight to drive.

Right from the start the rally engine produced 50 bhp and it didn't take long before 60 to 65 bhp was reached. This, in turn, caused problems with the

The first Saab to be used for rallying was this almost standard 92, with little more than additional lights to distinguish it from the normal specification.

79

Twenty-five years, as well as 225 horsepower, lie between these two Saabs, above. The company has always tried to compete with cars as close as possible to standard form, for development purposes. Here, below, is Erik Carlsson on his way to victory in the 1962 Monte Carlo Rally.

brakes. Erik Carlsson: 'The first time I realized this was during the 1957 Tulip Rally. The brake fluid couldn't cope with the temperatures and there I was, completely without brakes; that was a new experience for me!'

At the same time the shock absorbers started to cause problems. So far standard ones had been used, but now Mellde had to look for something better. The problem was solved when gas-filled dampers were introduced.

Maintaining the front-wheel-drive tradition, the 2-litre Saab 99 has proved to be a worthy successor to the famous 96 in international rallying, first in EMS form and more recently as the spectacular Turbo.

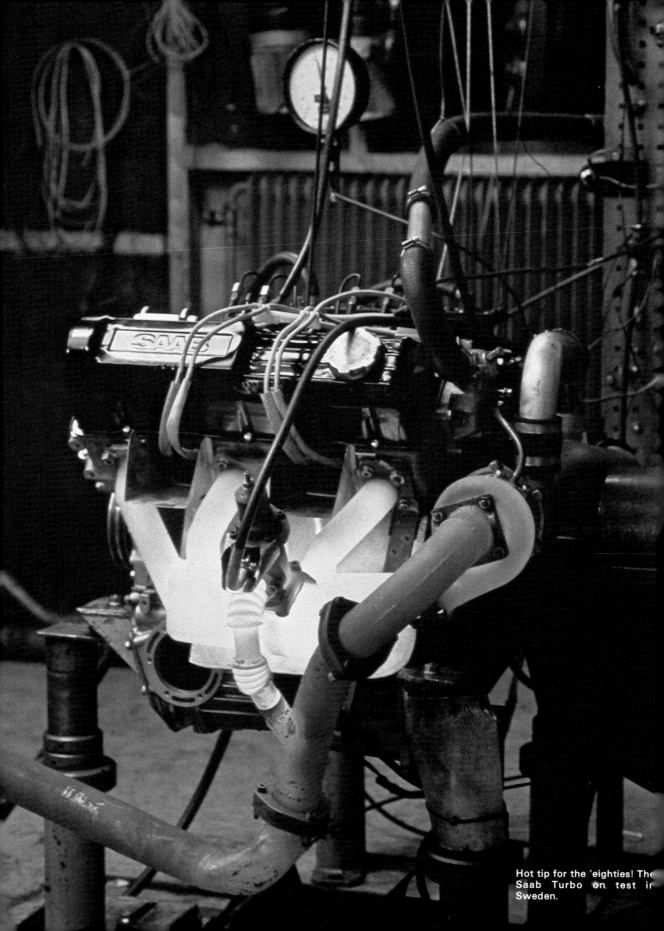

Hot tip for the 'eighties! The Saab Turbo on test in Sweden.

Experiments carried out on the Sonett I sports car resulted in an engine that produced 65 bhp. It was very difficult to drive, though, as it only pulled above 3,000 rpm, and then only for a couple of hundred revs. Driving in traffic was virtually impossible as you couldn't rev it properly and the plugs oiled-up.

For the 1959 Tulip Rally, Mellde provided Erik Carlsson with a Group 5 car, complete with four-speed gearbox, plastic wings and a 65 bhp engine. On the way out to the final test at Zandvoort the inevitable happened when the plugs fouled up in heavy traffic. But as the car was regarded to be in *parc fermé* Erik and his co-driver, Karl-Erik Svensson, could do nothing about it. Erik takes up the story:

'I have always had shrewd co-drivers. Karl-Erik read the regulations very carefully and when we reached Zandvoort he asked one of the other Swedish drivers to stay in the paddock for as long as possible before entering the circuit. He was to start in the same heat as we were, and the longer he

A close-up view of the cockpit and of some of the detail equipment of Carlsson's successful 1962 Monte Carlo Rally car.

FSTTT–6

A fully developed competition version of the Saab 96's V4 engine, left, makes a striking contrast with the standard product.

waited the more time we had to change the plugs at the start — which we were allowed to do. Exactly when I was ready he came out to start, and then I succeeded in beating the whole lot — including Harry Bengtsson's Porsche Super 90, which I passed on the last bend.'

Now Erik had what had been missing all the time in Saabs, the four-speed gearbox. It could only be used in Group 5, though, and that was the reason why Erik used a 95 for the 1960 Monte Carlo Rally.

However, the gearbox problem wasn't fully sorted until 1964, when the four-speed unit was homologated into Group One. In the meantime the front-end started to give trouble and a lot of work had to be put into it before it was working properly.

The rally cars were now based on the Saab Sport model and powered by an 841 cc engine, with separate lubrication. In competition form the engine produced 80 bhp, or nearly 100 bhp per litre. Two-strokes were easy to tune as they had very few moving parts, the biggest advantage coming from careful polishing of the ports and channels. Although it sounds easy, Bo Hellberg assures us it wasn't: 'You never knew how good an engine was until you ran it on the test-bed. Two engines

This overhead shot of the engine compartment of the standard Saab 96 V4 shows clearly the considerable amount of space which was available around the engine for special manifolding.

82

Another high-performance engine conversion for the V4 engine with long inlet trunking to the twin horizontal carburettors.

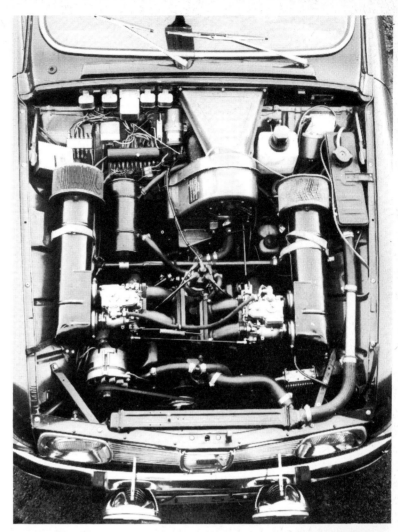

The Saab 99 was tried in rallies for the first time in 1974. Here is Lasse Jansson on one of the first stages in the Arctic Rally.

could look identical, one would run perfectly, while the other would have to be scrapped. The mechanics' skill and feeling for the job meant everything.'

Once the block was all right the next problem was choosing the correct carburettors, which wasn't easy. SAAB tried everything — horizontal carburettors, downdraught, single Solex, partly plugged double Webers; the list is endless. In its final form the 841 cc engine produced 84.5 bhp, but when bored out to 940 cc for the Formula Junior racer, power went up to over 100 bhp.

By 1966 the old two-strokes were pensioned-off

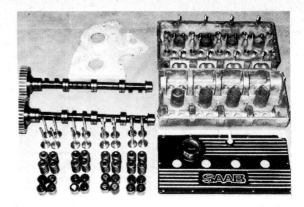

The 16-valve head for the 99 engine raised the power output to 225 bhp.

Stig Blomqvist won the Boucles des Spa first time out with the new car.

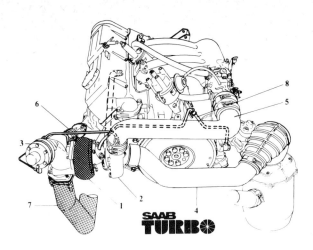

SAAB **TURBO**

in favour of the German Ford V4, which had powered their Group 3 Taunus in the Monte Carlo Rally. At that stage the 1.5 litre engine produced 90 bhp, which, according to Ford, was the maximum. Undeterred, the SAAB engineers got to work on the engine and soon found why the Germans were having problems getting more power — they weren't using the correct oil, and the engines simply exploded. A change of oil saw the engine tuned to produce 95 bhp with no reliability problems. In January of the following year, 1967, Åke 'the Brewer' Andersson and Torsten Åman won the Finnish Riihimäki Rally, which was the V4's first outright victory on a restricted international event.

There was plenty of space under the bonnet for

The introduction of the Turbo gave SAAB spectacular new possibilities in rallying, and by the end of 1979 the competition engine was developing 270 bhp. In this drawing of the turbocharged engine can be identified: 1-turbine; 2-compressor; 3-waste gate; 4-air filter; 5-air-fuel metering unit; 6-fuel by-pass; 7-exhaust manifold; 8-oil feed pipe. Right, the Turbo's engine compartment installation.

Stig Blomqvist puts a Saab Turbo through its paces in the snow.

the compact V4, but it drastically changed the car's weight distribution. Previously the ratio had been 59 per cent front and 41 per cent rear, but the figures now were 63/37. This encouraged the cars to understeer badly at every bend, while the springs and gearboxes initially couldn't take the strain and a lot of rapid development work was carried out before the problems were cured. Lessons learnt in the Competitions Department benefited the production cars as well, as they got stronger gearboxes, too.

SAAB has always used competition in order to improve the standard car, and being a small company it is relatively easy to get immediate feedback from the Competitions Department to the production line. When the last 96s were taken from the line to the Competitions Department not one single reinforcement had to be made — they were already in place thanks to knowledge gained in rallying. Of course bodies were changed on the Saab rally cars, but not because they were starting to fail. Rather, it was because certain drivers had a habit of rolling them every so often. . . .

By 1968 the search was on for more power from the V4; although it now produced 115 bhp that was still insufficient. The inlet manifold restricted the amount of petrol fed to the engine by the single twin-choke carburettor.

SAAB's rally drivers soldiered on with this problem until 1969, when the 1,740 cc US specification engine was homologated. Power was now up to 125 bhp, enough for Simo Lampinen to finish second behind Björn Waldegård's Porsche 911 in that year's Swedish Rally. But still the search was on.

Sigge Johansson, one of the Competition Department's top engine tuners, worked on a Lucas fuel-injection version and managed to get 181 bhp from a racing engine, but it lacked reliability, and even bringing the horsepower down for the rally cars didn't improve the reliability factor. Although the cars were very quick when the injection system worked, the fuel pumps couldn't supply the fuel all the time. The solution appeared in 1971 when a very sophisticated crossflow inlet manifold was homologated, allowing the use of twin-choke Weber 45 DCOE carburettors. Output immediately jumped to 145 bhp. Two years later SAAB homologated new cylinder-heads with separate outlets and this produced another 15 bhp. In its final form the engine produced 165 bhp, and Bo Hellberg thinks there was still more to come, but by now the car itself was getting outdated for rallying.

Back in 1969, SAAB had started to produce the larger 99 model and at the end of 1970 the Compe-

tition Department had begun to investigate its rallying possibilities, but the marketing people weren't interested and the 99 project was shelved until 1973. In that year a prototype was built with lower gearing, modified camshaft and two twin Webers, and in this relatively mild form the 99 was quicker over the test-track than a full-house 96 rally car.

Although the 99 didn't look a lot faster, it was smoother over rough surfaces than the 96 and put the power down a lot better. Neither did it turn over so easily!

The 99's rally debut came in 1974 when SAAB entered the Arctic Rally. Three cars were entered, a 96 each for Stig Blomqvist and Per Eklund and a silver 99 to be driven by newcomer Lasse Jansson.

The 99 was prepared to the then new Swedish Standard A regulations, which do not allow any tuning at all apart from blue-printing (carefully matching all the tolerances). SAAB did all they could to let people know it was a test car, going so far as to put 'Test 110 bhp' decals on the bonnet.

Jansson liked the car from the start, although with the handbrake operating on the front wheels it meant he couldn't do handbrake turns as in a 96. Nevertheless, after the first stage he was only 59 seconds down on Stig, who was leading the rally, and after five stages he was 15th overall. Jansson was then blocked by another competitor on a stage and had to put the car into a snowbank, which lost him quite a bit of time. Nevertheless, he fought on and, on one 25-mile stage, took 1 min 40 secs off Timo Mäkinen's Escort! His rally was to end on the 13th stage when the oil plug worked loose and the engine lost oil pressure, but the new car's debut could have been a lot worse.

Once back in Sweden, Lasse Jansson continued to use the car in the Swedish Championship and finished a respectable fourth overall at the end of the season. But it was becoming obvious that SAAB needed a new 2-litre rally car. The 96 was now only competitive in home events, for abroad Lancias, Renault Alpines and Ford Escorts were dominating the rally scene.

But in Trollhättan a new car was under way, and it was revealed to the press on December 17, 1975 — a Saab 99 EMS with twin overhead camshafts and 16 valves, producing 220 bhp. That was 50 more than SAAB had managed to squeeze out of the eight-valve engine. The car's competition debut came the following January when Stig Blomqvist drove it to victory in the *Boucles des Spa*, beating Dutchman Lars Carlson by more than six minutes after 600-odd miles of rallying.

The Belgian event, though, was only a test, as

were that year's Elba Rally and Welsh Rally — SAAB were aiming for the RAC in the following November, and they very nearly won it. With only half a dozen stages to go, Stig was fighting Roger Clark for the lead while Per was challenging for third place. But then disaster struck as Per's car suffered gearbox failure, ending his rally, and Stig had three punctures in a row, and had to be content with second place.

The 16-valve engine was used for two years, but then the FIA changed the rules and it would have meant building 400 power units to homologate the twin-cam. Unfortunately, SAAB couldn't afford the finance and to this day the twin-cam engines sit in the Trollhättan stores gathering dust. The 16-valve engine was one of the most reliable produced, and in four championship rallies Stig's engine wasn't even opened for an inspection.

At the Competitions Department, work had to start again on a new engine, and this time thoughts strayed to turbocharging. However, they were warned off this project as SAAB were undertaking tests with a production turbocharged engine and the marketing people didn't want anyone to draw conclusions from SAAB's competition turbo.

In late-1977, SAAB introduced the Turbo version of the 99 Combi Coupe and the Competitions Department were then given the green light to develop a rally version. Despite burning the midnight oil the car wasn't going to be ready for the 1978 Swedish Rally and so Stig did this event in a Lancia Stratos (SAAB-Scania import Lancias into Scandinavia), finishing fourth after mechanical problems and setting fastest times on nearly all the stages.

The Turbo made its competition debut in April, when Stig drove the car in the Esgair Dafydd Rallysprint where, in spite of two punctures, he finished fourth behind Hannu Mikkola (Ford Escort), Tony Pond (Triumph TR7 V8) and Russell Brookes (Ford Escort). In that year's RAC Rally both Stig and Per were destined to retire due to drive-shaft failure.

By the 1979 Swedish Rally, the two-door Turbo was homologated into Group 4 and Stig took a resounding victory over Björn Waldegård in a Ford Escort in a Turbo producing 250 bhp. A few months later this was upped to 270 bhp with no reliability problems. Stig's rallycross version produced 290 bhp — and there was more to come as the competition development of the Turbo continued to bring impressive results.

Chapter 16

Baja — 1,000 miles in 20 hours

In 1967 Erik Carlsson entered his last international rally, the Czech Vlatava Rally, or Rally Moldau as it is now called. Partnered by Torsten Åman, Erik won the event, thereby giving the Saab 96 V4 its first full international win. Then he quit rallying once and for all, except that in typical Erik fashion he made two comebacks. 'Although it had to be something really special,' Erik recalls, 'in a part of the world that I had never been to before.'

The scene of Erik's first comeback was the Baja 1000, run through the Southern Californian/Mexican peninsula of the same name. A Swede, Ingvar Lindqvist, who is a Saab dealer in Los Angeles, told SAAB of this peculiar desert race and how he had won the production class in his highly modified V4.

The idea sounded wild enough to Erik and, after he had seen a couple of films from the event, the decision was made; Erik was to compete in the Baja in a car prepared by Trollhättan. This is the story, as told by Erik's co-driver, Torsten Åman: 'The start took place in a town called Ensenada, some 60 miles south of Tijuana, the Mexican border town. Ensenada has a population of some 30,000 and marks the end of civilization; from there there is only one road, the "Mexican No 1" as it is called on the maps.

'The rules for the event are simple; just follow the main road from Ensenada to the finish in La Paz. For about 93 miles from the start there is no doubt that this is "Mexican No 1". The smooth tarmac road is very, very fast; Parnelli Jones was fastest in his Ford Bronco with a time of 1 hr 8 mins. Timing was rather loose as only the overall time counted. In between, competitors only had to pass through eight passage controls from the right direction.

'We couldn't beat Parnelli Jones' time, but we were very close, doing the first section only one minute slower. We thought that was pretty good as our top speed was only 105 mph and our average was 85 mph. We had done a lot of recce-ing and practice, and we used pace notes for the entire event, something that was unheard-of in this part of the world. Mind you, they helped.

'The first passage control was in Camalu, which also marked the end of the tarmac section. From there on the road was still wide and quite straight, but terribly rough. In places there were holes in the road big enough to swallow a car, and 'wash-outs' were frequent. These are dry river beds that cross the road, and they can be up to 12 ft deep and 45 ft across and with speeds up to 100 mph possible, are very dangerous if you don't know the road. Before we started our recce we were told numerous stories about vehicles approaching the dry river-beds at high speed and hitting the opposite bank head-on; one driver broke both his legs in such an accident.

'This notorious piece of road took its toll this year as well. Just after the Camalu control, two Bronco drivers tried to make up time after doing repairs. They jumped into their vehicle and set off without putting their helmets on or strapping themselves in. A few minutes later they met another vehicle in the dust and, to avoid a collision, took to a ditch where the Bronco turned over, killing them instantly.

'Dust is the biggest problem down there, and it is unavoidable with competitors starting at one-minute intervals. The second stage is 59 miles long and only the first third of it is relatively fast; after that the road narrows and gets progressively worse until you reach the second checkpoint at El Rosario, where the road virtually disappears. After

Erik Carlsson came out of retirement in 1969 to tackle the exotic Baja 1000 with a Saab 96 V4.

the second control you're in real Baja country where the road is nothing more than a feint line on a map.

'From here the road takes you through deserts and hills with hundreds of tracks, where it is very easy to get lost, before reaching the third control at Rancho Santa Ynez. By the time Erik and I reached here we had no idea where we were lying. Before the first control we had passed about 20 competitors, and about a further dozen by the second control, although you can never be certain as they are spread out between controls, trying to find the best route.

'This was very obvious between the second and third controls, as there were two main possibilities. One follows the route on the map, but is very bad, while the other follows an old caravan trail over the Red Mountains. The latter is narrow, steep and tricky, but shorter. It has one other advantage; we would be completely alone if we chose it, which we did. By the time we reached the third control at Santa Ynez there were only eight competitors in front of us, which was not bad considering we started at 82!

'Our Swedish mechanic, "Malin", was waiting for us at the control and changed the alternator,

which had been proving troublesome. Malin had a small 'plane at his disposal, which enabled him to be at virtually every check-point, as they were all situated at small airfields. At Santa Ynez there must have been about 160 aeroplanes present, all because of the race.

'We did about 10 miles after Santa Ynez when the car stopped with a split drive-shaft, right next to film star Steve McQueen's "Baja Boot", which had also broken down. By this time Malin had taken off from the previous control, but fortunately he spotted us on the road. We radioed him and told him of our trouble and he headed back to Santa Ynez where he borrowed a truck and drove out to help us repair the car, reaching us about an hour after we had originally contacted him.

'It should have been the end of the Baja for Erik and I, for the inner part of the shaft had broken and all the pieces were in the gearbox. Somehow, though, Malin fished them all out, and fitted a new shaft, then off we all went, Erik and I to the next control and Malin back to Santa Ynez, leaving Steve McQueen behind with his stationary 100,000-dollar special.

'As we drove along we tried to figure out what had happened and came to the conclusion that it

Mountains, deserts and dry lakes — the 'Baja' offers everything.

90

Essential modifications for the Baja 1000 included a substantial protective grille at the front of the car and twin fuel tanks.

'At this point we caught up with James Garner, who got a nasty shock when Erik asked him for a drink. Being a nice guy he obliged and gave us both some cold drinks before we set off again. The next section down to San Ignacio was relatively easy. For part of the way the twisty roads were smooth sand and we made maximum use of our pace notes and the Saab's 117 bhp. Our only slight problem was overtaking the other competitors, but they usually moved over when they saw us coming.

'We checked into the small oasis of San Ignacio at 1.15 am, knowing that the easy part was behind us. Ahead lay 150 miles of no-man's-land down to the seventh control at La Purissima. There are three different routes through this section: one over the mountains, a second that combines mountains and desert and, finally, the "beach" route along the coast. Most drivers choose the latter, but we took a chance on a very narrow, bumpy, but absolutely straight course through the desert and across a dry salt lake.

'We soon discovered the reason why we were the only ones taking this road; it was very difficult to

must have been due to the tyres. We had fitted larger tyres to get greater ground clearance and these had caused the drive-shafts to work under great stress at an acute angle.

'The repair had taken two hours and during that time we had been passed by several competitors including our team-mates, Ingvar Lindqvist/Sven Sundkvist and another film-star, James Garner. He was driving a very quick V8-engined Oldsmobile with a glass-fibre body.

'Those two hours also put our service schedule out of phase, as you aren't allowed to fly over the Baja after sunset and we had planned that Malin should reach the next control before dark, which, of course, he didn't do; this left us on our own all through the night.

'In spite of everything it all went smoothly down to the next control at Punta Prieta, where we caught up with Lindqvist. We tanked up and set off for the half-way stop at El Arco, where all the single-seaters and motorcyclists change drivers and riders.

Suspension modifications included double shock absorbers at the front of the car.

find and even more difficult to stay on. The trail split up every five minutes, like the fingers on a hand, and you had to be absolutely certain to take the right track otherwise you'd get lost or stuck in the sand. Once again, our careful preparation paid off for when the three routes converged there was no-one else in sight. We were leading!

'This happy state lasted for about an hour until 4.45 am, when the car stopped for a second time with a broken drive-shaft. We were stuck, 15 miles from the next control and in pitch darkness. After an hour, three motorcyclists came by and I gave each one three notes with the same message, "Please see that our practice car", which we knew should be at the next control, "is sent back to us", so we could take the parts needed from it.

'But nothing happened, and an hour later I hitched a lift from an old farmer who took me to the control, situated on top of a plateau with the obligatory airstrip. There was no practice car there, but I did manage to hire a 'plane and pilot who took me up to 5,000 ft where I reached Malin over the radio. Fortunately, he was airborne and heard my call and headed straight for us. An hour later we were back with Erik, and within 20 minutes Malin had got the car going again.

'Unfortunately, we had lost five-and-a-half hours and, in total, we were seven hours behind. Naturally, some drivers had passed us, but surprisingly few, although amongst them were Ingvar Lindqvist and James Garner. When I booked into the last check-point, Garner was still there servicing, and on seeing me he shouted to his service crew "There is that f-ing Swede again — hurry up!" But he had made a mistake, and thought we were the only ones to worry about, forgetting Ingvar Lindqvist completely. He thought as long as he kept his eye on us he could take his time and repair his very sick car.

'That was exactly what we had hoped for. Prior to the race we had decided to try and beat the old record of 20 hrs 38 mins, while Lindqvist plodded

Would you believe that this is Mexican Highway Number One?

on covering up for the team. At the finish Ingvar Lindqvist took his second straight win in the Production class, followed by James Garner and ourselves. A privately entered 99 finished in just under 50 hours, giving SAAB the team prize. We spent exactly 27 hrs 32 mins on the course, which meant we would have broken the absolute record if it hadn't been for the drive-shafts.

'But excuses, excuses. . . .

'When we left La Paz two days later there were still 11 vehicles missing, four motorcycles and seven assorted cars. Nobody seemed to know where to look, but funnily enough nobody seemed to be that worried. In Baja country you have to be able to look after yourself.'

Erik Carlsson and Torsten Åman went back the following year, this time accompanied by Pat Moss and Liz Nyström. But that's another story.

Chapter 17

Nobody drops a rear axle anymore

In 1953 Rolf Mellde won his one and only Swedish Championship, following victories in three of the qualifying rounds. This was the second year of the Championship, and it was to prove a very long time before a Saab driver clinched the title again. They all tried, Erik Carlsson, Carl-Magnus Skogh, Bengt Söderström, Olle Bromark and Ove Andersson, but they never quite made it.

But if they didn't win the Championship they did produce legends, some of which I have tried to recall in this book — trying to reveal the truth behind the screen of two-stroke smoke. In fact it wasn't until 1966 that Åke 'The Brewer' Andersson managed to take the title, this time in a Group 2 Saab 96, followed by Carl Orrenius, also in a Saab. During that year, the Swedish Federation decided to confuse everyone by running the Championship in two separate forms.

Until then the Championship had been run in 'Tillförlitlighet' (T), which means reliability. The events were run on secondary roads, although they were often very rough. Now the Federation wanted longer events on bigger roads, more like the Continental events, and thus a second Championship, 'Rally', was invented. In reality the two Championships were virtually identical, except that the rallies were longer than the T-events. Everybody realized that this was ridiculous, but nobody could do anything about it until 1972, when the controlling body, under pressure, changed the rules.

But perhaps SAAB gained something from this situation as they won another three titles in either works or semi-works cars. When Håkan Lindberg took the Group 1 title in 1968 he used his private car throughout. Only he and his father know how he made it.

By 1972 SAAB had had enough of the system and withdrew from the T-Championship, but still a Saab won; this time Åke Andersson took his privately-entered Group 2 car to the title. In all, Saab drivers took six Swedish T-Championship titles. When the Rally Championship was inaugurated in 1966, the Nordic Championship was well established and, in fact, Carl-Magnus Skogh had won the title. Stig Blomqvist emulated this in 1973, but nobody really took any notice as it was unofficial. The Swedish Rally Championship was to become very popular with drivers and the public alike, as everyone knew what it was, which is more than could be said for the T-Championship.

It was decided to run the Championship in two classes, Groups 1 and 2. At last, it was decided to permit the use of the tuned Group 2 cars that had existed all the time, but to which nobody had wanted to admit.

SAAB was very successful with three Championships and four seconds with the 96; Stig Blomqvist took the Championship in 1971, '73, '74, '75, '76 and '78, and Tom Trana in 1968. In 1974 the former Group 2 class was changed to the Special Class, but this didn't make any difference to Stig and SAAB, and in nine years Stig has won seven Championship titles.

But SAAB have also been very successful in the Standard classes that were introduced at the same time as the Special class, in 1974. Lasse Jansson took the brand new 99 to fourth overall in the Standard A class that year, and in the Standard B class untuned 96s have dominated completely.

The Standard A and B classes were introduced in an attempt to bring down the costs for privateers, but like many rules it failed in its purpose. The classes proved to be very popular, but as

Bo Hellberg, head of the Compe-
tions Department since 1962.

Stig Blomqvist, right, who made his
international competitions debut in
1965 with Torsten Palm, younger
brother of Gunnar.

expensive as ever to compete in. The 'A' class is for
cars with a power-to-weight ratio of 10–15 kgs per
bhp and the 'B' class for cars with more than 15 kgs
per bhp. Peculiar and typically Swedish!

Gradually, rallying has become more and more
professional in Sweden, and most privateers now
rely on sponsors and trailer their cars to and from
events. SAAB have tried to encourage private driv-

Erik Carlsson and Gunnar Palm, arguably the rallying world's first truly professional partnership.

ers and the results have been most worthwhile; in 1978, they won all three titles and by the end of 1979 Saab drivers had won 17 titles in all.

But this new-found professionalism does not produce the legends of the 'good old days'. In those times, the drivers had fun, pulling each other's legs and bragging about impossible stage times in the hope that their rivals would crash on a stage in an effort to equal fictitious times. Drivers would hit the headlines by rolling sideways at the end of a special stage, the co-driver using the next road section to kick the roof out again. As might be expected, Erik Carlsson has one such story. . . .

'On the 1957 1000 Lakes Rally we nearly lost the complete axle on one stage. But my co-driver, Mario Pavoni, managed to buy an entire welding kit from a blacksmith at the end of that stage. He then punched a hole in the floor from the inside, and while I took off for the next stage he was lying in the back, welding. Nice chap, Mario.'

The brain behind SAAB's professional attitude is Bo Hellberg, who was appointed head of Competitions in 1962. Two years later Bo Swanér, or 'Baby Bo', joined as his assistant and soon acquired a reputation as being one of the cleverest organizers in rallying. For example, on the 1979 Swedish

Rally he posted himself with one mechanic, a jack and two new tyres halfway through the rally's longest stage. 'We had calculated that it would pay off to change Stig's front tyres had they been worn out; they weren't needed though.' recalls Swanér.

The muscle through which the brains operate is in the shape of Stig Blomqvist, who was born in 1946 in Örebro, where he grew up with the late, great Ronnie Peterson. Not surprisingly, Stig passed his driving test on his 18th birthday (his father runs a driving school), and a few days later he entered one of his father's old Saab Sports in a local rally. The following year he entered the 1,000 Lakes Rally with Gunnar Palm's younger brother, Torsten, who went on to become one of Sweden's fastest single-seater drivers.

Stig didn't get an early breakthrough, though. It wasn't until 1969, when he was 23, that he gained support from Trollhättan and could develop into one of the world's great rally drivers. But legends? No, not with Stig around; for those you have to look to his ex-team-mate, Per Eklund.

Per is exactly the same age as Stig, but there the similarity ends. Stig is shy, almost withdrawn, whereas Per is open-minded and has a word for everyone, although he got himself something of a bad reputation when he kept rolling his car. Unfortunately for SAAB, they had to cut back on their competitions programme at the end of 1978, and

Workshop manager Paul Broman may never have been seen on a rally, but he knows exactly what the drivers require.

SAAB rally service in action at night and under less exacting conditions in broad daylight.

A comprehensive selection of spare parts are neatly and methodically packaged into a vehicle for maximum use of the available space.

during 1979 Per left to freelance, driving Triumphs, Porsches and Volkswagens with great skill and determination.

It is difficult for SAAB to compete against the larger companies who can spend fortunes on just one event, which is why SAAB pick and choose their events with care. But one thing is certain, they are every bit as professional as other teams, and in some cases more so.

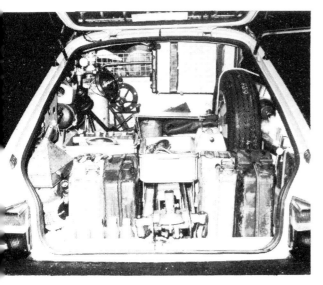

Bo 'Baby Bo' Swaner has the reputation for being one of the best organizers in the rally business. Above left, a full load of fuel and spares in a support vehicle.

SAAB never relied upon outside sponsorship until 1977, when a two-year agreement was signed with Polar Caravans, which was to be followed by a contract with Clarion, the Japanese manufacturer of high-quality car stereo equipment.

Three Swedish Champions. In 1978 the three titles went to Stig Blomqvist, Ola Strömberg and Per Eklund.

Chapter 18

Blue and white — for Finland

Saabs have been used for rallying in practically all parts of the world, from Mozambique to California, from Australia to Canada. Privateers and small sponsored teams have cropped up all over the place gaining inspiration from the works and achieving some good results. But in one country, Finland, the effort has been an almost continuous one for over 10 years.

In 1969, SAAB established an assembly plant at Uusikaupunki, in Western Finland, in conjunction with the dealer organization OY Scan-Auto, and it was decided that a Competitions Department should be included in the plans as well.

Saab cars were already established as rally winners in Finland long before the plant opened up, first by visiting Swedish drivers, then by a string of home-produced talent. The quickest of the local talent was Carl-Otto Bremer, who won the 1,000 Lakes, Hankiralli and the Finnish Championship in 1960. But unfortunately, Bremer was killed in an air-crash in the early-sixties and after him there was something of a vacuum. Although Rauno Aaltonen, amongst others, had cars loaned to them from Trollhättan the results didn't come, at least, not until Simo Lampinen came on the scene.

Simo, who will be remembered for his distinguished and polished style, had a difficult start. He was struck by polio at an early age, which left him with a bad limp, and the authorities granted him a driving licence at the age of 17 so that he could get to and from school.

But Simo wanted more than that, and as soon as he could, he obtained a competition licence and started rallying. Two years after his debut, in 1963, he won the 1,000 Lakes Rally and was Finnish Champion. He repeated his performance the following year, and in 1965 was Ice Racing Champion

as well.

This was exactly what SAAB needed in Finland, a Finnish driver who could get good results and could give the Swedes a fight on their home ground. When Simo won the RAC Rally in a Trollhättan-prepared car in 1968, his home town of Porvoo all but canonized him. But then Simo went to Lancia, and SAAB were left out on a limb.

In 1970, Scan-Auto prepared a blue-and-white 96 for Leo Kinnunen to drive in the 1,000 Lakes Rally, but he wasn't very successful and he and Scan-Auto soon parted company. Scan-Auto then changed tactics and decided to support young drivers, so that in the early-seventies you could find the likes of Jari Vilkas, Pertti Lehtonen, Robbi Gröndahl, Seppo Utriainen and Kai Alen (no relation to Markku) in the blue-and-white SAAB team cars. But this concentration on young talent turned out to be insufficient, as they couldn't give Scan-Auto the victories they wanted.

So, tactics were changed once again, and Simo Lampinen was tempted back to the fold. He immediately gave Scan-Auto what they wanted, and in 1972 he took his third victory in the 1,000 Lakes. In the preceding year, Stig Blomqvist became the third Swede ever to win the event, following in the tracks of Erik Carlsson (1957) and Volvo driver Gunnar Callbo in 1959. This was the beginning of Scan-Auto's domination of Finnish rallying that lasted until they pulled out in 1977. In 1972, the team consisted of Simo Lampinen, Tapio Rainio and Jari Vilkas, a trio that were virtually unbeatable — especially on the winter events.

Tapio Rainio won the Arctic Rally in 1974, followed by Blomqvist, the following year it was Lampinen's turn to lead Blomqvist home, and in 1976, when the rally finished in the northern town

Rauno Aaltonen was one of SAAB's Finnish drivers in the early-sixties, and Carl-Otto Bremer, far right, was the first Finn to be really quick in a Saab.

Leo Kinnunen and Timo Mäkinen were two fast drivers who made guest appearances in Saabs.

Tapio Rainio, Jari Vilkas and Simo Lampinen of the SAAB Finland team.

of Rovaniemi, it was Rainio's turn to collect the winner's laurels. SAAB completely dominated Finnish rallying, and in 1975, Saab drivers took the top three places in the Finnish Championship with Simo Lampinen taking his fourth title, followed by Rainio and Vilkas.

For 1976 the pattern was virtually the same.

Rainio won the Arctic for the second time, plus the Hankiralli, and went on to win the Championship, with Lampinen third and Vilkas fifth. In 1977 it was Stig Blomqvist's turn to win the Hankiralli, but this time in a car prepared for him by Scan-Auto. This is likely to prove the last big win for a Saab 96, and the combination of Stig and a

Finnish-prepared car underlines the co-operation there has been between Sweden and Finland during SAAB's competition history.

Following that particular rally, Scan-Auto built up two 16-valve 99s for Lampinen and Rainio to use in the 1,000 Lakes, but they were out of luck, as were the two works-entered cars for Blomqvist and Eklund. That proved to be the end of Scan-Auto's large-scale efforts, after which they started to support private drivers again, the most successful being Antero Laine. In 1977 he was Scandinavian Rallycross Champion in his black 96, and in 1978 and 1979 he was the sole driver to support SAAB's colours in Finland. Then, in a partial return to the big-time, for 1980 Scan-Auto built a Group 2 99 Turbo two-door for Stig Blomqvist to use on the Hankiralli, but unfortunately a fractured oil pipe brought his retirement when he was lying fourth.

Rallying at its best! This is the Finnish driver Tapio Rainio jumping his way to victory on the Arctic Rally.

Chapter 19

Good neighbours?

No foreigner has so far won the Swedish Rally. Simo Lampinen has been second three times, driving a Saab, naturally, and the very quick Norwegian, John Haugland, has been 10th in a Skoda. This is the closest that visitors from the east and west have been.

But the Swedes have been to both Norway and Finland and returned with victories, not always popular ones, either. When they are out of Scandinavia the drivers unite, but at home it's fight, fight, fight. I won't be accused of being too far from the truth if I say that the Finns and Norwegians have suffered some sort of inferiority complex in the past compared with the Swedish drivers, even though the Finns have since seemed to have a firm grip on the Swedes.

It has been debated whether Greta Molander was Norwegian or Swedish when she won the ladies' class in the Viking Rally as she was driving on a Swedish licence. Three years later it was Carl-Magnus Skogh who won the event, but after that it was Swedes who won Norway's premier event no less than ten times. Rallies have since been banned in Norway, but they used to be very tough, fast events, which meant that drivers had to go flat-out on the road sections. Norway's last important rally was the Soerland, which was won by Per Eklund.

For the Finns, rallying is an institution where the top drivers, like Hannu Mikkola, receive the same sort of adulation as footballers enjoy in England, and it is in Finland where there is the greatest rivalry between the Swedes and their Saabs.

If rallying in Finland is an institution, then the 1,000 Lakes is sacred — to the Finns it is the Cup Final, test matches and Wimbledon all rolled into one.

The correct title for the rally is the Jyväskylän Suurajot, or The Grand Prix of Jyväskylä, but it is normally called The Rally of the 1,000 Lakes, or just '1,000 Lakes'.

The first Swede to win it was Erik Carlsson, in 1957, when he was co-driven by the late Mario Pavoni. Pavoni was no better than anyone else at navigating, but he had a great ability to fix anything, anywhere. Nothing was too difficult for him, as he proved in that year's 1,000 Lakes.

'He spent most of the rally with a spanner in his hands,' Erik recalls. 'The worst time was when we bent the rear axle. We had no service along the route, just two spare wheels and a box of spark plugs — that's all. Obviously we couldn't change the rear axle, but Mario found a workshop in the middle of the night and, despite the fact that he couldn't speak a word of Finnish, he managed to borrow a carbide welding kit that must have been all of 50 years old. He grabbed it and went under the car to start heating up the rear axle before straightening it. I left him to it as the rear axle was right next to the fuel tank — but, fortunately, it didn't blow up.' Erik Carlsson won his class the following two years as well, but in 1960 it was Erik's turn to follow another Saab driver, and a Finn, Carl-Otto-Bremer, to the finish line.

Then the Finns found a new hero to follow in Rauno Aaltonen, an extremely good young driver, who was loaned a car by Trollhättan for some events. In 1961 he won the Hankiralli in a works car, followed by Carl-Magnus Skogh and Gunnar Palm, the latter making his debut with the SAAB team.

Despite the relative sophistication of rallying at this time, there were still some discrepancies as Skogh and Palm found out. Palm was getting

The SAAB team in the 1960 Thousand Lakes consisted of Carl-Magnus Skogh, Erik Carlsson and Carl-Otto Bremer.

The 'Finnish Grand Prix'. Stig tackles one of the special stages on the 1975 Thousand Lakes with absolute precision.

Simo Lampinen, second three times in the Swedish Rally, tackling the 1966 event.

Per Eklund has probably scored more wins in Norway than any other Swede. Here he is on the way to victory in the 1970 Sörland Rally.

Tom Trana, who drove Saabs from 1967 to 1972, won the Norwegian Rally in 1967.

Carl Orrenius and his co-driver Gustaf Schröderheim with the spoils of victory in the 1969 Hankiralli.

worried because his maps didn't look the same, and moreover he was right. Someone had given him a set of 1:100,000 and 1:200,000 scale maps!

In those days the Hanki was a long, tough event, and covering nearly 1,250 miles the route took competitors to the frozen north where the quicksilver wouldn't dare to climb the thermometers. It wasn't so much a question of rallying as surviving.

This didn't stop the young Aaltonen, though, and although he was leading Skogh he didn't have a comfortable margin until they reached his hometown of Turku, where he won two local stages. The following year, Skogh returned to Finland and won the event. In 10th place at the finish was a young driver on the threshold of a brilliant career, Simo Lampinen.

For eight years following Simo's win in the 1963 1,000 Lakes, the Finns dominated the event until a certain Mr Blomqvist turned up in his red 96 and won, much to the chagrin of the locals; the following year, however, they got their own back when Stig was penalized in a secret radar trap on a road section, thereby losing any chance of victory. Six months later he returned to win the Hankiralli for the third time in succession, while in 1977 he took a locally prepared Saab 96 to his fourth victory on the Hanki.

SAAB have a good record in Finland, their six 1000 Lakes victories up to 1979 being second only to Ford's seven.

But like any event the Jyväskylän Suurajot has claimed its fair share of spectacular spills. In 1969 Tom Trana and Sölve Andreasson left the road at high speed when Trana misjudged a slight right-hander. The roof was almost entirely ripped off by a tree and the spectators expected to find the worst. The only injury, though, was to Andreasson, who suffered a bruised finger nail! Some years later Per Eklund made a similar mistake and left the road at nearly 90 mph, hitting a bump and rolling the car forwards. Although his co-driver, Björn Ceder-berg, was taken to hospital for a preliminary check-up, Eklund was able to fly back to Sweden to compete in a hill-climb.

Finland has also been the setting for one of SAAB's rally-car debuts, the 99 in 1974. Stig Blomqvist drove a 16-valve 99 EMS on the 1000 Lakes, but did not finish. The sump guards proved too weak for the notorious 'yumps' and Stig retired after the first stage, followed by Per Eklund three stages later. Stig was annoyed about this as he was out for revenge after being caught for speeding during the previous year's 1000 Lakes. There is some mystery behind his supposed speeding as he was reported as having been driving a yellow 96, which was strange since the car was green. It might be explained by the fact that the previous year's car

Simo Lampinen and Klaus Sohlberg after victory in the 1972 Thousand Lakes.

was yellow. . . .

The fight between the Finns and the Swedes seems to be never-ending, and at the time of writing a Finn has yet to win the Swedish Rally. And who knows, it might be the Swedes' turn to win the next 1000 Lakes. No doubt the battle will go on for a long time to come. . . .

Chapter 20

Rallycross — all action

Most people now accept that rallycross was born in England in 1967 when that year's RAC Rally was cancelled due to the foot-and-mouth epidemic. Run for the TV cameras at Lydden Hill circuit, in Kent, it proved extremely popular with drivers and spectators alike.

In the autumn of 1971 the first event was held in Sweden at Hedemora, once the home of Grand Prix races in the 1950s. The Competitions Department in Trollhättan realized that this new, tough sport could be used to test developments for the rally cars, but the sport wasn't highly regarded by the Marketing Department; it was fine while the old 96 was used, but the new 99 was sacred and above the rough-and-tumble of rallycross.

Per Eklund emerged as SAAB's star in rallycross, battling against the VW Beetles which then reigned supreme, and often beating them. In 1973 the first unofficial European Championship was run, sponsored by Embassy cigarettes. Competition was fierce with cars like Jan de Rooy's Daf 66, complete with Ford BDA engine and gearbox, and John Taylor's works Ford Escort taking part. Blomqvist and Eklund had to compete against these highly sophisticated cars in their heavy and underpowered (165 bhp) Saab 96s. The following year, the organizers tightened the rules to make the cars less costly and specialized, which suited the Saabs, and Stig and Per finished third and fourth, respectively, in the Championship. Although the placings weren't the best, it is estimated that some 227,000 spectators attended the 38 rallycross meetings that year in Sweden alone. The cars were being seen — that was important.

In 1974, Sweden's *Rallysport* magazine organized a local championship, which was won by Lasse Nyström in his turbocharged VW Beetle,

with Stig finishing fourth and Per sixth overall. Their placings might have been higher if it hadn't been for the intense rivalry between the Saab duo, which resulted in barging matches much to the spectators' delight.

By now the 96s were getting rather long in the tooth, and in 1975 Eklund could only finish fourth in the Swedish Championship, while in the European Championship Stig finished 14th and Per 17th. By 1976, however, the turbocharged 96 engine was ready, and its arrival coincided with the first official Swedish Championship. In that year's final it was Saab versus Porsche, the German cars being driven by Björn Waldegård and Sune Jansson. Against all the odds the little Saabs put up a

Today's rallycross cars are highly modified with a completely stripped interior braced by a substantial roll cage.

tremendous fight, but victory eventually went to Waldegård, followed by Stig and Jansson, with Per having to settle for last place following a drive-shaft failure at the end of the race.

Per followed up this performance with 10th place in the European Championship, while Stig was fifth in the Dutch Championship. Stig then opted out of rallycross for a few years to concentrate on developing the 99 Turbo rally car, although he has since acquired a 290 bhp rallycross version of the two-door Turbo, while Per continues to participate in the sport with a turbocharged 96 which, at the last check, was producing 200 bhp.

When rallycross became popular in Sweden competitors used regular rally cars and Per Eklund was still a young man!

Pat Moss-Carlsson made a guest appearance on one of Trollhättan's rallycross cars in the Chamonix ice race in 1973.

Stig Blomqvist started to use the 99 Turbo in rallycross in 1979 and its 290 bhp proved more than sufficient to hold off the opposition in the championship finals.

A tight battle between a Saab and a VW typifying the closeness of competition in rallycross.

Finnish driver Antero Laine campaigned his private Saab 96 in rallycross with very good results during 1977 and 1978.

Rallycross can be a rough sport at times with spectacular crashes and plenty of work to do between races in the pits.

Over page, Per Eklund was one of the first Swedes to realize that rallycross could be fun . . .

Chapter 21

From Little Le Mans to Showroom Stocks

SAAB's early competition attempts in America were a very low-key effort, although the performance of the little two-strokes in the 1,500-mile American Mountain Rally, where they won the manufacturers' prize, encouraged the new importers (SAAB Motors Inc.) to pursue an active competitions policy, realizing that competition not only improved the breed, but also gained much needed publicity for their new product. Those early two-strokes seemed ideally suited to racing and it wasn't long after the Saab's first appearance in America that they were being raced by enthusiastic amateurs.

In 1957, the promoters of the then newly opened Lime Rock Park circuit (Connecticut), held the first Little Le Mans 12-hour endurance race for imported cars. A miniature version of the French classic, the Lime Rock race featured a Le Mans-type sprint start, pit stops and tyre changes and attracted numerous personalities including TV newsman Walter Cronkite, band leader Paul Whiteman and restaurateur Vincent Sardi.

Another feature of the race was the requirement to use standard road tyres, which necessitated the pit stops. By the end of that first race, it was estimated that each car had used nearly 100 tyres — considerably more than the sponsors, the Sports Car Club of America, had reckoned on. In fact, the situation became so desperate at one stage that some of the spectators had to 'volunteer' tyres from their cars so that their favourites could continue racing.

That first 12-hour race, held in October round the 1½-mile Connecticut circuit, boiled down to an all-Swedish contest with the larger 1.6-litre Volvo 544s taking the top five places, followed by four Saabs. The Index of Performance trophy, based on engine displacement, speed, fuel consumption, etc., as well as the class prizes, went to SAAB. For the SAAB team, the Index of Performance became a standard prize in virtually every Little Le Mans race held since 1957, the 93 being the winning car until 1962, when the 96 was introduced. From 1957 to 1963 Saabs were class-winners every year, and usually finished in the top six overall as well.

The race was cut in length from ten hours in 1958 to eight hours in 1959, but this did not upset the SAAB domination of the Index of Performance, even if the outright winners changed from year to year. In 1958 it was still a Volvo/Saab battle, but the following year some very rapid 750 cc Fiat-Abarth Zagatos took the top places while in 1960 a Studebaker Lark (believe it or not) was the overall winner. By 1963 the event had moved to the Marlboro (Maryland) circuit, where the previous year a 12-hour race had been staged in which a Saab shared by Mayforth and Braun had survived a first-hour roll to finish second to the winning Volvo P544. The 1963 event, however, was dominated by Fords, with Cortinas finishing first and second and a Falcon third, although Saab 96s did well in coming home fourth (Mayforth/Thompson) and fifth (Andrey/Rutan).

As is so often the case in motorsport, some of those early Saab drivers in the Little Le Mans races went on to bigger and better things. Gaston Andrey, a Swiss-born racer and Boston Saab dealer, drove in every single Little Le Mans, but has subsequently won five national SCCA championships in Ferraris, a Morgan Plus-4 and a Birdcage Maserati. Clyde Billing, of Washington, Maine, was another who made a name for himself, this time at ice-racing, and in 1957 he opened a Saab dealership in his home town.

But perhaps the most famous name to emerge from those early days is Roger Penske, who has subsequently found fame and fortune as a Can-Am, USAC and sometime-F1 entrant, as well as running a very successful chain of Chevrolet dealerships and is also a big diesel-engine and truck dealer. Bob Holbert, of Warrington, Pennsylvania, competed in Saabs at Little Le Mans before going on to race Porsches and drive in the Can-Am for the Shelby team. He passed on his skills to his son, Al, who has since made a name for himself racing Porsches and Chevrolet Monzas in SCCA and IMSA racing.

As happened in Europe, Saabs soon became favourite cars for enthusiastic amateurs, with the dealers in Maine, New Hampshire and Vermont entering cars in local ice races. The front-wheel-drive two-strokes were at an immediate advantage over their rivals in this class of racing and, while speeds may not have been spectacular, it was cheap and good fun for all concerned. The premier event was a six-hour endurance ice-race held at Brunswick, Maine, where Saab dealers would compete amongst themselves. Front runners in this class were the Billing family, with Clyde driving, his wife Harriet organizing the service (and sometimes driving as well), and their three sons, Mike, Peter and Butch, doing the service and relief driving. It was quite a family affair, especially as they won the

A tyre change and refuelling stop during the 1957 Little Le Mans.

race on no less than four occasions!

SAAB's involvement with track racing in the United States took a rather low profile until 1976, when the executive editor of *Car and Driver* magazine, Pat Bedard, decided to race a fuel-injected Saab 99 GL in the magazine's 'Challenge V' held at Lime Rock Park race circuit. The *Car and Driver* Challenge was started in 1971 by the magazine, and it provided the magazine's staff with the opportunity to race at the Connecticut circuit against invited readers, advertisers, etc. The editorial staff usually emerged as winners, with Pat Bedard (who subsequently achieved some

The Le Mans-type start in 1957 seemed to be a more leisurely affair than what used to happen in the French classic!

112

One of the Saabs being chased hard by a Volvo in the 1958 Little Le Mans.

No time to lose during a pit stop for a somewhat battered Saab in the 1959 race. By the look of his overalls the driver had found it pretty hot work!

Two wheels on a Saab provides a tighter line than all four wheels on an NSU Prinz during the 1959 Little Le Mans.

success in big NASCAR stockers and endurance Ferraris) as one of the front-runners.

Bedard had been impressed with the 99's overall handling characteristics when he had test-driven the car for the magazine. His belief in the car was further strengthened by Glenn Seureau, a Saab dealer from Houston, Texas, who had started racing his 99 EMS with considerable success. Bedard borrowed an EMS from SAAB-Scania of America for the Lime Rock race, little realizing that his chief opponent would be Stig Blomqvist, who was flown over specially for the event. In order to race legally, Blomqvist became a member of the New England region of the Sports Car Club of America, and the holder of an SCCA licence. However, on race day, Blomqvist nearly failed to start as his helmet did not conform to American regulations,

and there was a frantic panic as SAAB personnel searched for, and eventually found, a helmet for him. From the start of the race, a battle developed between Stig and Pat Bedard, with the talented American heading Blomqvist on three occasions before the race was brought to a premature halt by an accident when Stig was running first and Bedard second.

The Saab one-two marked the start of the company's current involvement with American Show-room Stock racing. By the start of the 1977 racing season, SAAB's American PR Manager, Len Lonnegran, also found himself appointed as Competitions Manager, with a team of factory racers to look after. SAAB's three-car team used experienced Showroom Stock drivers, headed by Don Knowles, a budget analyst for the US Secretary of

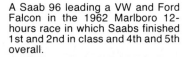

Understeering strongly, one of the Saabs striving to keep up with an Alfa Romeo Spider at Lime Rock in 1963.

A Saab 96 leading a VW and Ford Falcon in the 1962 Marlboro 12-hours race in which Saabs finished 1st and 2nd in class and 4th and 5th overall.

Don Knowles in close combat with another Saab driver in the 1978 Showroom Stock run-offs at Road Atlanta.

Agriculture in Washington, Jon McKnight, Associate Dean of Students at Rutgers University, New Jersey, and PR man Bill Fishburne. Even before the racing season got under way, though, the trio made their first mistake:

The SCCA appointed an *ad hoc* Showroom Stock Committee, made up of drivers (including some of the Saab drivers) to clarify rules and the eligibility of cars. At their first meeting, they were faced with the proposition that the Saab 99 be moved from Showroom Stock A to Stock B. In order to stop this the Saab drivers offered a compromise and allowed all Alfa Romeos to remain in SSB, thinking of the Alfetta saloons and forgetting the Spider sports car. Consequently, Saab drivers had to get used to losing races in the 1977 season to the very quick Alfa Romeo Spiders, which were not only winning the SSB class, but also the races outright. The first official National Championship was held in the October of that year, and although seven Saabs qualified for the final, the headline from an Alfa poster tells the story: 'One of the drivers overslept . . . Alfa finishes 1, 2, 3, 4, 5, 6, 7, 8, 9 . . . Saab 10'.

Because Showroom Stock rules allow only one, two or three-year-old cars to compete, the 1974 Alfa Romeo Spiders were barred from racing in 1978 and this opened the floodgates to the Saab drivers, who dominated the class throughout the season, some 30 of them competing in the series

throughout the United States, including the three works drivers, who had been joined by Tom Walker, a marketing expert from Seattle. Eventually, 11 Saabs made it to the Road Atlanta final, following some 75 races throughout the United States, which had resulted in nearly 50 first places in the SSB class alone.

Despite the presence of a few Alfetta GTs at the finals, Saab drivers claimed the top eight places on the grid, following a somewhat harrowing week of

SAAB's first US national racing champion, Don Knowles on his way to victory.

115

practice, during which two Saabs were written-off. Bill Fishburne rolled his car five times, while Knowles succeeded in getting his car sideways, too. Fortunately, there were Saabs in the paddock (for emergencies such as these), and after some long nights of work both drivers had cars for race day. Fishburne's wrecked car was eventually donated to the SCCA as a 'Crash and Burn' school wreck.

When the flag dropped for the final, Don Knowles shot off into the lead, while the other Saab drivers ganged-up on the few Alfettas that were competing, and after that it was simply a question of which Saab would finish where, behind Don Knowles. Eventually, Royce Wray, an American airline pilot from Chicago, was second, followed by Tom Walker, with David Grunwaldt, a dentist from Green Bay, Wisconsin, fourth and Bill Fishburne, fifth. The best non-Saab finished sixth.

For the 1979 season, the Saab 99 Turbo (intro-duced the preceding year) became eligible for Showroom Stock A, thus giving Saab two bites of the cherry — SSA and SSB. Over 40 drivers campaigned Saabs actively throughout the country, with the 1978 champion, Don Knowles, driving both a 99 GL as well as a 99 Turbo. By virtue of his 1978 championship, Knowles was automatically eligible for the 1979 championships provided he entered three SSB races during the season. This he did, duly winning two, while in the third he ran half the race and then parked his car, enabling other Saab drivers to get enough points to qualify for the finals; 20 Saab drivers eventually qualified for the Road Atlanta meeting.

As they had in 1978, SAAB took over a large area of the paddock and rented a marquee so that their cars could be serviced under cover. In addition, they brought along a large truck full of spares — the importers were taking this racing seriously and meant to win — while one of the more enterprizing drivers got a large blimp with

Don Knowles leads Ron Christensen's Mazda RX3 in the 1979 Road Atlanta Showroom Stock B final.

Knowles and his crew show the victor's flag during a lap of honour after winning his second Showroom Stock B final at Road Atlanta in 1979.

A Saab Turbo leads a Porsche 924 through the Esses at Road Atlanta.

US national SSA champion Ron Christensen fighting a pack of Datsuns, Porsches, Saabs and a Chevrolet Monza at Road Atlanta in 1979.

'SAAB' written on it, and floated it over the Swedish company's camp.

Despite all their effort, though, the Saab drivers were hard pushed to take overall honours. In the SSA race, a quasi-works Porsche 924s and Datsun 280Zs proved to be considerably quicker than the Saabs on the straights, although the Swedish cars made up for that on the bends. The only trouble was that Road Atlanta has more straights than bends . . .

Fortunately, though, the Porsches and Datsuns got tangled up near the end of the race, and for the second year in succession the Saabs became the National Champion cars.

The 1979 Showroom Stock B final was hotly contested between Saabs, Mazda RX3s and a few Alfetta GTs, and leading the Saab brigade was reigning champion and race favourite Don Knowles. Eventually, Knowles came good, but not until he took to the grass to get past some slower cars, which moved him up into first place, where he finished. Second across the line was Ron Christensen, who had forsaken Saab for a very quick Mazda.

At the awards banquet after the last race, Ron Christensen, of Salt Lake City, Utah, took the SSA prize in a three-door 99 Turbo while Don Knowles had won the SSB with his 99 GL.

The hard luck Professor

Jon McKnight is a highly respected member of the SCCA. Apart from being an accomplished racing driver, he also instructs at SCCA drivers' schools and is an active SCCA official — he is also SAAB's hard-luck man.

During his Showroom Stock racing days, he usually drove his Saab to and from Rutgers University, where he worked. That is, until he rode a friend's motorcycle one mid-summer day in 1979 and was involved in an accident with a car. Although his injuries were minor, confined to bruises and sprains, it was enough to keep McKnight out of racing for several weeks.

McKnight had qualified second for the 1978 race, but decided to alter his tyre pressures before

Hard-luck man Jon McKnight in the rain at the Pocono Raceway, Pennsylvania, in a 1978 Showroom Stock event.

the flag dropped. He shouldn't have bothered, as it upset the car's handling, causing him to spin at one point and eventually finish a lowly seventh.

The year 1979 was kinder to the Professor, or so it seemed. He started the Showroom Stock A final well up the grid and eventually took over the lead from Don Knowles when the latter was forced to retire, at about half-distance, with piston failure; this was a problem that had reached almost epidemic problems for the Turbos during practice and qualifying, and both Fishburne and Walker had retired from the race with the same fault. McKnight eventually took the chequered flag, although not before fighting for the lead with two Porsches and a Datsun who got past him only to collide with one another. McKnight was followed across the line by fellow Saab Turbo driver Ron Christensen.

McKnight's problems had only just started, though, for the next day he was disqualified and Christensen was declared the winner. A technical inspection had found that McKnight's fuel was of the wrong specific gravity and, although McKnight admitted to using an octane booster, he claimed that SCCA rules allowed it (he was backed up on this point by several fellow drivers). Nevertheless, the decision stood, and Christensen collected the prizes.

After the inspection, McKnight had the fuel analysed and discovered that it contained 20 per cent alcohol, something he had never put in. It is now believed that the mysterious alcohol was the cause of a spate of piston failures which befell six Saab Turbos.

Chapter 22

Into the 'eighties

Although 1979 might have finished on something of a sour note when both Stig Blomqvist's and Ola Strömberg's Saab 99 Turbos retired on the RAC Rally, the team bounced right back again in their first rally of 1980. The first round of the Swedish Championship, the Bergslagsrally, was utterly dominated by Saabs, Blomqvist winning outright in his Turbo, followed home by Lasse Jansson in his 150 bhp 99 EMS, who also won the Standard A class. Further down the field was Kalle Grundel in his 90 bhp Saab 96, with which he won the Standard B division.

SAAB's first International of the year was the Boucles de Spa; the last time SAAB had won this event was with Stig Blomqvist driving the twin-cam version of the 99 EMS. This time, the factory had something else new to offer their number-one driver — power steering. Although power steering has been tried on rally cars before, the systems used have proved too insensitive and slow to respond. However, SAAB's system is based on the Saginaw power unit, as used on the road-going 900 series, and in tests it was found to decrease stage times by a second per kilometre. Not only does power steering reduce the drivers' effort, but it also allows the use of wider tyres, especially racing slicks for tarmac events. The effectiveness of the new system was immediately underlined by Stig's fine first place, some six minutes ahead of his nearest rival 'Didi' in his Fiat 131 Abarth.

Stig Blomqvist raises a snow cloud on a special stage during the 1980 Swedish Rally, his Turbo displaying sponsorship by the Japanese stereo equipment manufacturer Clarion.

119

SAAB now consider the International Swedish Rally and the RAC Rally as the two most important events in their competition calendar. The 1980 Swedish was, perhaps, more important than ever, as the team wanted to underline the effectiveness of the Turbo as a rally car following its convincing win on the preceding year's event. Right from the start, the rally turned into a battle between Stig and Anders Kullang in the new Opel Ascona 400. Unfortunately, a puncture robbed Stig of victory by a mere 90 seconds, but his proved to be the drive of the rally.

SAAB's next outing in the European Championship was at the other end of Europe, on the Costa

Stig Blomqvist and Björn Cederberg on their way to second place overall on the 1980 Swedish Rally.

Intense concentration by the Blomqvist/Cederberg partnership as their Saab Turbo tackles a ford on the Boucles de Spa in Belgium.

Spectacular cornering by Blomqvist on a dusty stage during the Costa Smeralda, when once again he finished in second place overall.

Heads down for Blomqvist and Cederberg for a tight corner on another dusty stage on the 1980 Costa Smeralda.

Smeralda. Predominently a gravel-stage rally, it presented Blomqvist with tough opposition from the likes of Bernard Darniche in his Lancia Stratos. Nevertheless, Stig put up a magnificant show to finish second, just over four minutes behind the flying Frenchman. Shod with Pirelli tyres instead of the more normal Dunlops, Stig didn't suffer from a single tyre failure — something of a record. Even Darniche was surprised by the competitiveness of the car, and was glad he ran number-one on the road so that Stig had had to drive through his dust clouds.

Perhaps Stig's toughest victory in the 1980 season came on the South Swedish Rally, which counted towards both the Swedish and European Championships. Although Stig led from start to finish he was hard-pressed by the Opel Ascona 400 of Björn Johansson and had the added problem of losing first, third and reverse gears after 25 of the 38 stages. Stig's winning margin was a mere 13 seconds!

Some success came in Britain during the annual televised Rallysprint in which Stig drove the Saab Dealer Team-sponsored car into third place behind the TR7 V8 of ex-teammate Per Eklund and winner Pentti Airikkala (Vauxhall Chevette 2300 HS).

Meanwhile, over in America, SAAB continued their domination of production car racing when a 900 Turbo three-door driven by Bill Fishburne, Don Knowles and *Road and Track* journalists John Dinkel and Joe Rusz won the 'Longest Day' 24-hour Showroom Stock race held at Nelson's Ledge, Warren, Ohio.

It looks as though SAAB are starting the 'eighties, where they began the 'fifties, 'sixties and 'seventies — competing with enthusiasm and dedication . . . and winning!

The hard-charging Saab Turbo of Fishburne, Rusz, Knowles and Dirkel, outright winners of the 1980 Longest Day 24-hours race for Showroom Stock cars in the United States, which continued the Swedish company's fine record in this class of racing.

A summarized survey of SAAB rally results

Year	Rally	Result
1951	Swedish Rally to the Midnight Sun	1st, ladies class
1952	Monte Carlo Rally	1st, ladies class
1953	Tulip Rally	1st, ladies class
	Swedish Rally to the Midnight Sun	1st, ladies class
	Viking Rally	1st, ladies class
	Swedish Championship	
	European Rally Championship	1st, ladies class
1955	Tulip Rally	1st, ladies class
1956	Viking Rally	1st, ladies class
	Wiesbaden Rally	1st overall
	Tour d'Europe Continental	2nd overall
	Great American Mountain Rally	1st overall
	Rally de Corse	1st overall
1957	Viking Rally	1st, ladies class
	Finnish Rally	1st overall
	Acropolis Rally	2nd overall
	Adriatic Rally	1st overall
	European Rally Championship	1st overall
1958	Monte Carlo Rally	2nd, ladies class
	Sestriere Rally	1st, ladies class
	Swedish Rally to the Midnight Sun	1st, ladies class
	Great Florida Rally	1st overall
	Viking Rally	1st, ladies class
	Lourenco-Marques Rally	2nd overall
1959	Canadian International Rally	1st overall
	Swedish Rally to the Midnight Sun	1st overall
	Wiesbaden Rally	1st overall
	West Flandre Rally	1st overall
	Viking Rally	2nd overall
	German Rally	1st overall
	Portuguese Rally	4th overall
1960	Circuita da Fortalesa	2nd overall
	Finnish Snow Rally	1st overall
	Swedish Rally	1st overall
	Rally 500	1st overall
	Finnish Rally	1st overall
	Polish Rally	2nd overall
	Viking Rally	1st overall
	RAC Rally	1st overall
	Acropolis Rally	2nd overall
	Nordic Championship	1st
1961	Canadian Winter Rally	1st overall
	Finnish Snow Rally	1st overall
	Norwegian Winter Rally	1st overall
	Acropolis Rally	1st overall
	Monte Carlo Rally	4th overall
	Swedish Rally to the Midnight Sun	1st overall
	Polish Rally	2nd overall
	Rally of the Thousand Lakes	4th overall
	RAC Rally	1st overall
	Nordic Championship	1st
1962	Monte Carlo Rally	1st overall
	Tulip Rally	4th overall
	Acropolis Rally	2nd overall
	Swedish Rally to the Midnight Sun	3rd overall
	Rally of the Thousand Lakes	3rd overall
	RAC Rally	1st overall
	Finnish Snow Rally	1st overall
	Canadian Winter Rally	3rd overall
	East African Safari Rally	3rd overall
1963	Monte Carlo Rally	1st overall
	Rally of the Thousand Lakes	1st overall
	RAC Rally	3rd overall
	Canadian Winter Rally	3rd overall
	Finnish Snow Rally	2nd overall
	Norwegian Winter Rally	3rd overall
	Swedish Rally to the Midnight Sun	2nd overall
	Vltava Rally	1st overall
	Spa-Sofia-Liège	2nd overall
1964	Monte Carlo Rally	3rd overall
	Rally de Fiori	1st overall
	East African Safari Rally	2nd overall
	Coupes des Alpes	2nd overall
	Polish Rally	2nd overall
	Spa-Sofia-Liège	2nd overall
	Geneva Rally	2nd overall
1965	Monte Carlo Rally	3rd overall
	Swedish Rally	2nd overall
	Acropolis Rally	2nd overall
	Polish Rally	3rd overall
	Gulf Rally	2nd overall
	RAC Rally	3rd overall
1966	Swedish Rally	1st overall
	Norwegian Winter Rally	1st overall
	Tulip Rally	1st in class
	Acropolis Rally	1st in class
	Gulf Rally	1st in class
	Vltava Rally	1st in class
	Rally of the Thousand Lakes	1st in class
	Coupes des Alpes	1st in class
	Lyon-Charbonnière	1st in class
	Geneva Rally	1st in class
	Rally Volta a Portugal	1st in class
	Ethiopian Highland Rally	2nd overall
	Angola Rally	1st overall
	Rally of Libya	1st in class
	Malaysian Rally	1st overall
	Swedish Championship	1st
1967	Riihimaki Rally	1st overall
	Swedish Rally	2nd overall
	Norwegian Winter Rally	1st overall
	Finnish Hankiralli	1st overall
	Scottish Rally	3rd overall
	Gulf Rally	4th overall

	Vltava Rally	1st overall
	Rally of the Thousand Lakes	2nd overall
	Norwegian Rally	1st overall
1968	Swedish Rally	2nd overall
	Finnish Hankiralli	1st overall
	Norwegian Winter Rally	1st overall
	Scottish Rally	4th overall
	Gulf Rally	3rd overall
	Vltava Rally	2nd overall
	Rally of the Thousand Lakes	2nd overall
	Norwegian Rally	1st overall
	RAC Rally	1st overall
	Swedish Championship, T	1st
	Swedish Championship, Rally	1st
1969	Norwegian Winter Rally	1st overall
	Finnish Hankiralli	1st overall
	Riihimäki Rally	1st overall
	Scottish Rally	1st overall
	Gulf Rally	1st overall
	Norwegian Autumn Rally	1st overall
	Baja 1000	3rd overall
	RAC Rally	2nd overall
1970	KAK Rally	2nd overall
	Norwegian Winter Rally	1st overall
	Norwegian Sörland Rally	1st overall
	Swedish Championship	1st
1971	KAK Rally	1st overall
	Finnish Hankiralli	1st overall
	Norwegian Winter Rally	1st overall
	International Police Rally	1st overall
	Rally of the Thousand Lakes	1st overall
	RAC Rally	1st, 3rd, 7th and team
	Swedish Championship, Rally	1st
	Swedish Championship, T	1st
	Irish Rally	1st (Group 2)
1972	KAK Rally	1st overall
	Finnish Hankiralli	1st overall
	Rally of the Thousand Lakes	1st overall
	Swedish Championship, T	1st (Group 2)
	RAC Rally	2nd overall
	Scandinavian Championship	1st
1973	Bergslagsrally	1st overall
	KAK Rally	1st, 2nd overall
	Finnish Hankiralli	1st, 3rd overall
	Swedish Championship, Rally	1st, 2nd and 3rd
	Cyprus Rally	1st
1974	Arctic Rally	1st, 2nd overall
	Jemt Rally	1st, 2nd overall
	European Rallycross Championship	3rd, 4th overall
	RAC Rally	2nd overall
	Swedish Championship, Rally, Special Class	1st
1975	Bergslagsrally	1st, 3rd overall
	Riihimäki Rally, Finland	1st, 2nd overall
	Arctic Rally, Finland	1st, 2nd, 3rd overall
	KAK Rally	2nd, 4th overall

	Finnish Hankiralli	1st, 2nd, 4th overall
	Rally of the Thousand Lakes	2nd, 4th overall
	Swedish Championship, Rally, Special Class	1st, 2nd
	Finnish Championship, Rally	1st, 2nd, 3rd
1976	Bergslagsrally	1st overall
	Boucles-de-Spa, Belgium	1st overall
	Arctic Rally, Finland	1st overall
	International Swedish Rally	1st, 2nd overall
	Finnish Hankiralli	1st overall
	Sachs-Baltic Rally, Germany	2nd overall
	Munich-Vienna-Budapest Rally	2nd overall
	Car and Driver Challenge, Lime Rock, USA	1st overall
	RAC Rally	2nd overall
	Swedish Championship, Rally, Special	1st overall
	Finnish Championship, Rally	1st overall
1977	Bergslagsrally	1st overall
	Swedish Rally	1st overall
	Perce Neige Rally, Canada	1st overall
	Finnish Hankiralli	1st overall
1978	Castrol International Rally, Australia	2nd overall
	Piston-les-Wapitis, Canada	1st overall
	La Jornada Trabajosa, USA	1st overall
	Baise des Chaleurs, Canada	1st class, 2nd overall
	Swedish Championship	1st (Group 4)
	Swedish Championship, Standard A	1st
	Swedish Championship, Standard B	1st, 2nd
	National Championship in Showroom Stock, USA	1st, 2nd, 3rd, 4th 5th
1979	Swedish Rally	1st overall
	Mintex Rally	1st overall
	Ulster Rally	3rd overall
	Rallysprint (TV)	2nd
	South Swedish Rally	1st overall
	Little Le Mans, USA	1st overall
	Baja 1000	1st class
	Canadian Championship Rally	1st Production class
	National Championship in Showroom Stock, Class A, USA	1st
	National Championship in Showroom Stock, Class B, USA	1st
	Swedish Championship, Standard B	1st
1980	Bergslagsrally	1st overall and 2nd overall
	Boucles-de-Spa, Belgium	1st overall
	Swedish Rally	2nd overall
	Rally Costa Smeralda, Italy	2nd overall
	South Swedish Rally	1st overall
	Longest Day, 24-hour Showroom Stock Race, USA	1st overall
	Rallysprint (TV)	3rd overall

Saab rally car standard specifications

Saab 92 (1950–55)

Engine: Transverse, two-cylinder, two-stroke. Water-cooled without pump. Capacity: 764 cc. Bore/stroke: 80 × 76 mm. Compression ratio: 6.6:1. Max power: 25 bhp at 3,800 rpm. Max torque: 41 lb ft at 2,350 rpm. Single downdraught Solex carburettor. Four per cent petroil blend.
Transmission: Front-wheel drive; three-speed gearbox, second and third with synchromesh. Dry clutch.
Brakes: Eight-inch drums all round. Brake area: 91.9 in. Mechanical handbrake acting on rear wheels.
Steering: Rack-and-pinion. Turning circle: 36 ft. Wheels: 3½J × 15. Tyres: 5.00 × 15.
Suspension: Individual shock absorbers with transverse torsion bars front and rear.
Electrics: Six-volt battery, 80–90 Ah 130 W generator.
Dimensions and weight: Length, 154.3 in. Width, 63.7 in. Height, 55.9 in. Wheelbase, 97.2 in. Track, 46.4 in. Ground clearance, 6.7 in. Kerb weight, 1,686.5 lb. Tank capacity, 7.7 galls.
Top speed: 62–65 mph.
Model changes: 1953, Saab 92B introduced with larger rear window and boot lid added. 1954, fitted with 28 bhp engine, re-styled wheels and chrome trim.

Saab Sonett Super Sport (1955–56)

Engine: In-line, three-cylinder, two-stroke. Water-cooled (competition version had total-loss system). Capacity: 748 cc. Bore/stroke: 66 × 73 mm. Compression ratio: 10:1. Max power: 57.5 bhp at 5,000 rpm. Max torque: 69 lb ft at 4,500 rpm. Single downdraught Solex carburettor. Three per cent petroil blend.

Transmission: Front-wheel drive; three-speed gearbox, second and third with synchromesh. Dry clutch.
Brakes: Nine-inch drums at front, eight-inch drums at rear. Brake area: 105 sq in. Mechanical handbrake acting on rear wheels.
Steering; Rack-and-pinion. Turning circle: 32 ft. Wheels: 4J × 15. Tyres: 5.00 × 15.

Suspension: Coil springs all round, solid beam rear axle.
Electrics: 12-volt battery, 33Ah 160W generator.
Dimensions and weight: Length, 138 in. Width, 53.9 in. Height, 32.5 in. Wheelbase, 86.6 in. Track, 48 in. Ground clearance, 4.3 in. Kerb weight, 1,102 lb. Tank capacity, 11 galls.
Top speed: 103-plus mph (depending on gearing).

Saab 93 (1956–59)

Engine: In-line, three-cylinder, two-stroke. Water-cooled with pump. Capacity: 748 cc. Bore/stroke: 66 × 73 mm. Compression ratio: 7.3:1. Max power: 33 bhp at 4,200 rpm. Max torque: 52 lb ft at 3,000 rpm. Single downdraught Solex carburettor. Three per cent petroil blend.
Transmission: Front-wheel drive; new three-speed gearbox, second and third with synchromesh. Dry clutch.
Brakes: Nine-inch drums at front, eight-inch drums at rear. Brake area: 105 sq in. Mechanical handbrake acting on rear wheels.
Steering: Rack-and-pinion. Turning circle: 36 ft. Wheels: 4J × 15. Tyres: 5.00 × 15.
Suspension: Coil springs all round with solid beam rear axle.
Electrics: 12-volt battery, 33 Ah 160 W generator.

Dimensions and weight: Length, 158.0 in. Width, 62.0 in. Height, 58.0 in. Wheelbase, 98.0 in. Track, 47.2 in. Ground clearance, 7.5 in. Kerb weight, 1,775 lb. Tank capacity, 7.9 galls.

Top speed: 68 mph.

Model changes: 1958, Saab 93B. Whole windscreen, indicators, three per cent petroil mixture. New ignition coil. March 1958, Saab 750 GT with 45 bhp engine, improved front seats, smaller rear seat, sports steering wheel, tachometer, speedpilot, twin chrome side-stripes. Tuning kit available for competition purposes increasing engine output to 45 bhp (Stage 1) or 55 bhp (Stage 2).

Saab 95 (1957–78)

Engine: In-line, three-cylinder, two-stroke. Water-cooled with pump. Capacity: 841 cc. Bore/stroke: 70 × 73 mm. Compression ratio: 7.3:1. Max power: 38 bhp at 4,250 rpm. Max torque: 59 lb at 3,000 rpm. Single down-draught Zenith carburettor. Three per cent petroil blend.

Transmission: Front-wheel drive; new four-speed gearbox, synchromesh on all forward gears. Dry clutch.

Brakes: Nine-inch drums at front, eight-inch drums at rear. Brake area: 105 sq in. Mechanical handbrake acting on rear wheels.

Steering: Rack-and-pinion. Turning circle: 36 ft. Wheels: 4J × 15. Tyres: 5.60 × 15.

Suspension: Independent front, coil springs all round, solid beam rear axle.

Electrics: 12-volt battery, 34 Ah 300 W generator.

Dimensions and weight: Length, 162 in. Width, 62 in. Height, 58 in. Wheelbase, 98 in. Track, 48 in. Ground clearance, 7.5 in. Kerb weight, 2,000 lb. Tank capacity, 9.5 galls.

Top speed: 79 mph.

Model changes: 1964, new nose increased overall length by seven inches. 1965, further external changes made, and special version of 95 introduced in America

and Switzerland with more powerful Monte Carlo engine, front disc brakes and revised dashboard including tachometer. 1967, V4 version introduced (engine details as 96) although two-stroke versions still available. 1968, two-stroke had 46 bhp engine for all markets except USA. 1969, larger grille and different rear-light cluster fitted. 1970, improved facia and minor controls, new seating arrangement and uprated front shock absorbers. 1974, new grille and improved anti-corrosion treatment adopted. 1976, 95 provided with 99's impact-absorbing bumpers. Third row of seating at back eliminated. 1977, fitted with front seats of 99 and engine uprated by 3 bhp to 68 bhp.

Saab 96 (1960–66)

Engine: In-line, three-cylinder, two-stroke. Water-cooled with pump. Capacity: 841 cc. Bore/stroke: 70 × 73 mm. Compression ratio: 7.3:1. Max power: 38 bhp at 4,250 rpm. Max torque: 59 lb ft at 3,000 rpm. Single down-draught Zenith carburettor. Three per cent petroil blend.

Transmission: Front-wheel drive; three-speed gearbox, second and third with synchromesh. Dry clutch.

Brakes: Nine-inch drums at front, eight-inch drums at rear. Brake area: 105 sq in. Mechanical handbrake acting on rear wheels.

Steering: Rack-and-pinion. Turning circle: 36 ft.

Wheels: 4J × 15. Tyres: 5.60 × 15.

Suspension: Independent front, coil springs all round, solid beam rear axle.

Electrics: 12-volt battery, 34 Ah 300 W generator.

Dimensions and weight: Length: 162 in. Width, 62 in. Height, 58 in. Wheelbase, 98 in. Track, 48 in. Ground clearance, 7.5 in. Kerb weight, 1,810 lb. Tank capacity, 8.5 galls.

Top speed: 75 mph.

Model changes: 1960–62, GT 750 version with 748 cc (66 × 73 mm) engine with triple carburettors, compression ratio 9.8:1, max power 45 bhp at 4,800 rpm, max torque 61 lb ft at 3,500 rpm. 1962–66, GT 850 version (known as Saab Sport in UK and Monte Carlo in USA) with 841 cc (70 × 73 mm) engine with triple carburettors, compression ratio 9:1, max power 55 bhp at 5,000 rpm, max torque 68 lb ft at 3,800 rpm. Front disc brakes standard. 1963, four-speed gearbox optional on 96 models.

Saab Sonett II (1966–69)

Engine: In-line, three-cylinder, two-stroke. Water-cooled with pump. Capacity: 841 cc. Bore/stroke: 70 × 73 mm. Compression ratio: 9:1. Max power: 60 bhp at 5,200 rpm. Max torque: 69 lb ft at 4,000 rpm. Triple horizontal carburettors. Three per cent petroil blend.

Transmission: Front-wheel drive; four-speed gearbox, synchromesh on all forward gears. Dry clutch.

Brakes: 10.5-inch discs at front, 8-inch drums at rear. Brake area: 256 sq in. Mechanical handbrake acting on rear wheels.

Steering: Rack-and-pinion. Turning circle: 35 ft. Wheels: 4½J × 15. Tyres: 155 SR 15.

Suspension: Independent front, coil springs all round, solid beam rear axle.

Electrics: 12-volt battery, 34 Ah 300 W generator.

Dimensions and weight: Length, 148 in. Width, 58 in. Height, 45 in. Wheelbase, 84 in. Track, 48 in. Ground clearance, 7 in. Kerb weight, 1,565 lb. Tank capacity, 13 galls.

Top speed: 100-plus mph.

Model changes: 1968, two-stroke engine dropped in favour of V4, although performance unchanged. Column gear-change dropped in favour of floor-mounted lever. External changes included power bulge on bonnet to accommodate larger engine, and rubber overriders.

Saab 96 V4 (1967–79)

Engine: V4, four-cylinder, four-stroke. Water-cooled with pump. Capacity: 1,498 cc. Bore/stroke: 90 × 58 mm. Compression ratio: 9.0:1. Max power: 65 bhp at 4,700 rpm. Max torque: 85.8 lb ft at 2,500 rpm. Single FoMoCo downdraught carburettor.

Transmission: Front-wheel drive; four-speed gearbox, synchromesh on all forward gears. Dry clutch.

Brakes: 10.5-inch discs at front, 8-inch drums at rear. Brake area: 256 sq in. Mechanical handbrake acting on rear wheels.

Steering: Rack-and-pinion. Turning circle: 35 ft. Wheels: 4½J × 15. Tyres: 155 SR 15.

Suspension: Independent front, coil springs all round, solid beam rear axle.

Electrics: 12-volt, 44 Ah battery, 35 Ah alternator.

Dimensions and weight: Length 169 in. Width, 62 in. Height, 58 in. Wheelbase, 98 in. Track, 48 in. Ground clearance, 5 in (with two front passengers). Kerb weight, 2,050 lb. Tank capacity, 8.5 galls.

Top speed: 88–91 mph.

Model changes: Monte Carlo V4 produced in 1967, with standard engine but same trim as two-stroke Monte Carlo.

1968 models had larger windscreen and windows all round. General improvements to interior. Monte Carlo dropped, De Luxe introduced. 1969 versions had different grilles with rectangular headlamps, plus exterior changes. Vacuum servo fitted to brakes. 1970, more exterior improvements and facia re-designed. Rear seat improved and De Luxe model dropped. Headlamp wash/wipe system fitted. American-specification V4s had 1.7-litre engine and 8.0:1 compression ratio, power output unchanged at 65 bhp. Heated driver's seat fitted to all cars. New gearbox casing developed from rally cars and fitted to production models in 1975.

Saab Sonett III (1969–74)

Engine: V4, four-stroke. Water-cooled with pump, Capacity: 1,698 cc. Bore/stroke: 90 × 66.8 mm. Compression ratio: 8.0:1. Max power: 65 bhp at 4,700 rpm. Max torque: 85.8 lb ft at 2,500 rpm. Single FoMoCo downdraught carburettor.

Transmission: Front-wheel drive; four-speed gearbox, synchromesh on all forward gears. Dry clutch.

Brakes: 10.5-inch discs at front, 8-inch drums at rear. Brake area: 256 sq in. Mechanical handbrake acting on rear wheels.

Steering: Rack-and-pinion. Turning circle: 30.8 ft. Wheels: Cast aluminium, 4½J × 15. Tyres: 155 SR 15.

Suspension: Independent front, coil springs all round, tubular beam rear axle.

Electrics: 12-volt, 44 Ah battery, 35 Ah alternator.

Dimensions and weight: Length, 160 in. Width, 59 in. Height, 47 in. Wheelbase, 84.6 in. Track, 48.5 in. Kerb weight, 1,875 lb. Tank capacity, 13 galls.

Top speed: 100-plus mph.

Model changes: 1972, new black plastic grille fitted, rear panel painted black. Wider-section aluminium wheels adopted. 1974 version fitted with 99-type bumpers and headlamp wipers.

Saab 99 (1969–to-present)

Engine: In-line, four-cylinder, four-stroke. Water-cooled with pump. Capacity: 1,709 cc. Bore/stroke: 83.5 × 78 mm. Compression ratio: 9.0:1. Max power: 80 bhp at 5,200 rpm. Max torque: 94 lb ft at 3,000 rpm. Single Zenith-Stromberg carburettor.

Transmission: Front-wheel drive; four-speed gearbox, synchromesh on all forward gears. Dry clutch.

Brakes: 10.6-inch discs front and rear. Brake area: 351 sq in. Mechanical handbrake acting on front wheels.

Steering: Rack-and-pinion. Turning circle: 33 ft. Wheels: 4½J × 15 in. Tyres: 155 SR 15.

Suspension: independent front, coil springs all round, rigid rear axle with Panhard rod.

Electrics: 12-volt, 60 Ah battery, 35 Ah alternator.

Dimensions and weight: Length, 171 in. Width, 66 in. Height, 57 in. Wheelbase, 97.4 in. Track, 54.7 in (front), 55.1 in (rear). Ground clearance, 6.7 in (unladen). Kerb weight, 2,400 lb. Tank capacity, 9.9 galls.

Top speed: 95–99 mph.

Model changes: Spring 1970, three new models introduced including Saab's first four-door. Automatic transmission available with Bosch D-Jetronic fuel injection, 87 bhp at 5,200 rpm and 95 lb ft torque at 3,000 rpm. 1971, engine size 1,854 cc by increasing bore to 87.0 mm; carburettor version 88 bhp at 5,000 rpm and 108 lb ft torque at 3,000 rpm; fuel-injection version 95 bhp at 5,200 rpm and 105 lb ft torque at 3,200 rpm. 1972, 1.7-litre engine discontinued. 99 EMS introduced with fuel-injected engine and manual gearbox in two-door bodyshell. Engine outputs raised by 2 bhp, bore increased to 90 mm, capacity 1,985 cc. Outputs for carburettor and fuel-injected engines 95 bhp at 5,200 rpm, 115 lb ft torque at 3,500 rpm and 110 bhp at 5,500 rpm, 123 lb ft torque at 3,700 rpm, respectively. 1973, single-carburettor version using Stromberg 175 CD producing 95 bhp at 5,200 rpm and 116 lb ft torque at 3,500 rpm. 1974, 165-section tyres replaced 155s and power-steering available in some markets. Saab Combi Coupe introduced, a true hatchback 110 mm longer than conventional saloon but with estate-car-carrying capacity when needed; 12-gallon fuel tank. 1975, Bosch D-Jetronic fuel injection replaced by Bosch constant-injection mechanical system; saloons received 12-gallon fuel tank. European versions of Combi Coupe with twin-carburettor engine producing 108 bhp at 5,200 rpm and 121 lb ft torque at 3,300 rpm. 1976, five-door Combi Coupe announced with opera window. Fuel-injected, automatic four-door revealed as GLE top-of-the-range model. September 1977, Saab 99 Turbo three-door introduced. 1,985 cc engine using Garrett AiResearch turbocharger with standard block, crankshaft and con-rods. New pistons, compression ratio reduced from 9.2:1 to 7.2:1. Final-drive ratio altered. Power increased to 145 bhp at 5,000 rpm and 174 lb ft torque at

3,000 rpm. 1978 model range, EMS and GLE only available in three- and five-door shells, respectively. Saab 99s now only as two- and four-door saloons with single- or twin-carburettor engine and automatic gearbox. 1979, turbocharged version of 99 two-door introduced. Engine specification as for three-door Turbo.

Saab 900 (1978–to-present)

Engine: In-line, four-cylinder, four-stroke. Water-cooled with pump. Capacity: 1,985 cc. Bore/stroke: 90 × 78 mm. Compression ratio: 9.2:1 (Turbo, 7.2:1). Max power: 100 bhp at 5,200 rpm, 119 lb ft torque at 3,500 rpm (single carburettor); 108 bhp at 5,200 rpm, 121 lb ft torque at 3,500 rpm (twin carburettor); 118 bhp at 5,500 rpm, 123 lb ft torque at 3,700 rpm (fuel-injected); 145 bhp at 5,000 rpm, 174 lb ft torque at 3,000 rpm (turbocharged).

Transmission: Front-wheel drive; four-speed manual gearbox, five-speed manual on Turbos and option on others. Three-speed automatic also available. Synchromesh on all gears. Dry clutch.

Brakes: 11-inch discs at front, 10.6-inch discs at rear. Brake area: 387 sq in. Mechanical handbrake acting on front wheels.

Steering: Rack-and-pinion. Turning circle: 33.8 ft. Wheels: 5J × 15, 5½ × 15 HZ (three-door Turbo), 35/TRX 390 FM (five-door Turbo). Tyres: 165 SR 15, 175/70 HR 15, 195/60 HR 15 or 180/65 HR 3901.

Suspension: Transverse wishbones, coil springs and hydraulic shock absorbers (front). Dead rear axle with four longitudinal links, Panhard rod, coil springs and hydraulic shock absorbers (rear).

Electrics: 12-Volt, 60 Ah battery, 72 Ah alternator.

Dimensions and weight: Length, 186.6 in. Width, 66.5 in. Height, 55.9 in. Wheelbase, 99.4 in. Track, 56.3 in (front), 56.7 in (rear). Ground clearance, 5.9 in. Kerb weight, 2,650 lb. Tank capacity 12.1 galls.

Top speed: 105-120-plus mph depending on engine specification.

Model changes: Five-speed gearbox available in Saloon version of 900 announced August 1980, four-door versions with twin-carburettor, fuel-injected or turbocharged engines. Automatic version of Turbo available.